INDIANA WRITING PROJECT
DEPARTMENT OF ENGLISH
BALL STATE UNIVERSITY
MUNCIE, IN 47306-0460

THE SPITTING IMAGE

Garth Boomer
Dale Spender

Rigby Limited, Adelaide
Sydney • Melbourne • Brisbane • Perth

First Published 1976
Copyright © Garth Boomer and Dale Spender
All rights reserved
Set in Australia by Avant Garde Photocomposition, Adelaide
Printed in Hong Kong

This book is copyright. Apart from any fair dealing for
the purpose of private study, research, criticism, or
review as permitted under the Copyright Act, no part
may be reproduced by any process without written permission.
Inquiries should be made to the publishers.

National Library of Australia cataloguing in publication data.

Boomer, Garth
   The spitting image.

   ISBN 0 7270 0162 0.

    1. Language and languages — Addresses, essays,
   lectures. I. Spender, Dale, joint author. II. Title.

Contents

Preface
1. It's the Middle Class which loses ... 1
2. Piggy nick—that's a good word ... 8
3. It's all a question of floral arrangement (or How to fail school on day one) ... 17
4. More guesses equals freedom ... 22
5. Good grade three sentences and a joining word ... 27
6. You've just got to be able to tell ... 40
7. Who has the language deficiency? ... 44
8. There is no such thing as linguistic sin ... 50
9. Why can't they be like me? ... 53
10. How many languages do you need? ... 58
11. How to stop kids reading ... 62
12. Wanking with words ... 68
13. Don't let anyone know your secret (or The language of universities) ... 73
14. Give up imitations and try the real thing ... 78
15. A steaming heap of jargon: the language of the new education ... 82
16. Have you thought about sex lately? ... 88
17. It's all done with mirrors ... 98
18. The sociolinguistic interface ... 104
19. Do teachers really know what they are asking? ... 110
20. Scratch an education expert 118
21. Who's afraid of the illiteracy scare? A personal view ... 124
22. Please don't take this personally ... 132
23. I've got to be me ... 141

Acknowledgements

Illustrations

Cover	Ron Langman Photography
Page 19	Times Newspapers Limited, London
Page 23	© 1975 United Feature Syndicate, Inc., Sydney
Page 48	© Field Newspaper Syndicate, Chicago
Page 54	Times Newspapers Limited, London
Page 64	Times Newspapers Limited, London
Page 70	Michael Leunig, "Nation Review", Sydney
Page 79	Michael Leunig, "Nation Review", Sydney
Page 89	Michael Leunig, "Nation Review", Sydney
Page 100	Michael Leunig, "Nation Review", Sydney
Page 106	Bruce Petty, "The Australian", Sydney
Page 112	© 1970 United Feature Syndicate, Inc., Sydney
Page 137	Michael Leunig, "Nation Review", Sydney

Preface

"But schools declare themselves as surely as people do. And children learn to read the implicit meanings more quickly and thoroughly than they learn many prescribed tasks. 'What does this place say to me?' they ask and look for the answer in every intonation of the institution. In finding the answer they also discover what it is possible for them to say."*

We believe that many children learn hypocrisy at school, from teachers who wittingly or unwittingly deny their own voices to be in accord with the "intonations of the institution." We also believe that schools and universities often limit possibilities for saying things by failing to admit or to take account of the ways in which language is used "out there." A fear of linguistic pollution seems to possess so many classroom vigilantes in this country. Ironically, these people would almost certainly see themselves as fighters in the cause of literacy just when, in fact, they are killing off meaning and communication with every raised eyebrow and every "tut tut." Of course, those who learn to be right and acceptable, if not honest, are the academic winners, ready now to perpetuate linguistic capitalism.

And so, this is not a neutral book. It is not objective; nor is it always coherent in theme and intention although you will no doubt detect a pervasive irreverence for institutional closed doors and good table manners. Sometimes we hope to raise a laugh.

We are two voices, easily distinguished, reflecting, not always in tranquillity, on some things we have read and done and observed mainly in schools and universities and departments of education. We suggest that the chapters might be taken piecemeal as the mood takes you because that is how we wrote it. Much of our writing is anecdotal. At times we call on theory explicitly but generally the theory is implicit or so assimilated as to be unrecognizable. Anyway, we are entirely responsible for any irresponsibility.

As touchstones, untarnished by our world views, we offer three transcripts, one of the monologue of a three year old boy, one of a dialogue with a seven year old school girl and one of the voice of a grandfather long since removed from school. Those who find our critical appraisal of schools, teachers, universities and educational "experts" a little negative in spirit may re-kindle a positive flame by returning to these records of the living language.

Unaccustomed as we are, we think we have some things to declare. We hope you will let at least some of them in.

R.G.B.
D.S.
Adelaide and London, 1976.

*Connie and Harold ROSEN, *The Language of Primary School Children,* Penguin Education, London, 1973, p. 21.

It's the Middle Class which loses! 1

There is always
Someone
Waiting there to detect
The error.
Waiting for you
To prove
That you have not quite
Caught on
The way they have.
There is always
Someone
Waiting to score.

It used to be
The teacher,
Who would smile
Disdainfully
When he told me
That a preposition
Was not a good word
To end a sentence
With.
And I listened
Carefully,
And I practised
Carefully
Until I got it
Right.

2 THE SPITTING IMAGE

I still have to think
Carefully
But I do not
Make that error
Any more.

Then it was
Another teacher
Who would smile
Disdainfully
At my use of the
Subjunctive.
And I listened
Carefully,
And I practised
Carefully,
Until I could say
"If I were"
As though it were
The natural thing
To say.
So I got it
Right
And I do not
Make that error
Any more,
Either.

Then there was
The lecturer
Who would smile
Disdainfully
When I did not know
The right jargon
And I "split" my infinitives,
And my style
Was too gauche,
But I listened
Very carefully,
And I practised
Very often,
Until I could
Sound as he did.
Of course it meant

That I had to think
Carefully,
Before I ever spoke,
And it meant
That I did not speak
If I could avoid it.
But eventually,
I became like him
And I too
Could smile
Disdainfully
At those lesser creatures
Who had not yet
Got it right!

And then it was
The parents
Of my fiancee
Who would smile
Disdainfully
When I said "tea" for "dinner"
And "savouries" for "Hors d'Ouvres".
But I was always
On my guard
And listened
Carefully
To this new brand
Of rightness.
And I was very quiet
Until I had learnt
All the new terms.
And now, I get them
Right, too.

After that it was
The boss' wife
Who would smile
Disdainfully
At *everything* I said,
And it took
Quite some time
To determine
What the trap was
Into which I was

4   THE SPITTING IMAGE

Falling,
But I realized
The error of my ways
And found that it was
My vowel sounds.

So I listened
Carefully,
And practised
Perfectly
And I spoke
Infrequently,
Until I got them
Right.

And then it was
My secretary
Who would smile
Disdainfully
When she brought
The letters in
For me to sign.
And that proved quite
A challenge.
And I had to look
Secretly
At the correspondence
Of the Director
To see how it was done,
So that I would not fall
Into the trap.
But I read
Carefully
And I practised
Carefully,
Until I got it
Right.

Every day
There seems to be
Someone
Who knows more
Than I do,

Someone,
Who has learnt
All the secrets,
Someone
Who is waiting
Ready to smile
Disdainfully
Whenever I open
My mouth
Or begin to write.
And everyday
Of my life
I try so hard
To get it right.
I have a rule
To think three times
Before I speak.

When I get into bed
At night,
I go over everything
I have said
During the day,
And recall the reactions
Of those to whom
I have been speaking
To see if I did fall into
Any traps.
And there is always
Some rule
I have not thought of
Before
And it is a constant
Pressure.
And I become very angry
With myself
That I have not been
More careful,
That I have not been
Quick enough
To learn them all
Yet.

6 THE SPITTING IMAGE

I have progressed
Far
From the manner
In which I used
To speak.
I have come
A long way.
I have achieved
Well.
My own parents
Have difficulty understanding me
At times.
And I have learnt
To smile
Disdainfully
At their ignorance.
They neither listen
Nor practise.
They are not
Cautious speakers
As I am.

But surely the day
Must come
When I do know
All the rules
And I can begin
To speak
With confidence.
The day must come
When I know
There are no new rules,
When I have them
All right.
When I will not have to
Undergo this inward
Detection process
With my words
Before I give them
Utterance.

Surely
The day must come
When I know all
The pitfalls
And I can
Negotiate them all
And not be
The victim
Of disdainful smiles!
Surely . . .

I do not talk
As much as I used to.

2 Piggy nick — that's a good word

Simon and Catherine and Jean and I were living in a one bedroom garret in a three storey block of flats in London. We'd been in England only a couple of weeks and I noticed that Simon's pre-sleep monologues had grown to proportions which would have done credit to Cecil B. de Mille. He'd been in the habit of talking to himself back in Australia but the transplant to London seemed to have given his bedtime spiel a new impetus.

Unethically, but in the interest of science, I decided to do a Watergate on him. I planted a tape recorder behind the bedhead. The night-time ritual was to put Catherine and Simon down in the double bed while Jean and I read or watched television in the "lounge". When it was our bedtime we had to transfer the children to makeshift beds in the lounge.

Catherine, who was then five years old, always dropped off to sleep very quickly, leaving Simon, then 38 months, alone with himself. On the night of the second of October 1972 his only "property" was his teddy bear. Catherine was asleep alongside him.

What follows is my transcript of what he said. The tape, which I still keep as a precious document, is available as confirmation that I have not "doctored" what was said other than to give an orthographic approximation for some of the sounds.

* * *

(*Simulated sleep noises*)
   Pssh . . . Pssh . . .
(*10 second silence*)
   Scratch . . .
(*assorted sounds*)
(*2 minutes silence*)
   Prr
   Daddy's the boss, daddy's the boss, daddy the daddy is the boss (*chanted*)

(*indistinct sentence*)
(*20 second silence*)
   The water bag
   The hot water bag   (*Catherine has taken a hot water bag to bed*)
(*laughing*)
   Hallo, Hallo, Halloo, Halloo, Halloo
   Yup the up the poo
   Jiggety, jiggety jog
   The mouse ran up the clock
   The mouse ran down
   Jiggety, Jickety — (*pause*) jock
(*mumbling, then 1½ minute silence*)
   Is that Greg or Nanna or Grumpy or Alison
                                  (*his cousin, back in Australia*)

   I haven't got any honey
   Do with it to do with it
(*indistinct sounds*)
   That won't hurt
   Look at that
   P' yoopy, yoopy, yoopy, yoop
(*indistinct whispering*)
   Sit down, sit down (*dramatized*)   (*earlier that day, Simon had
   Why you crying   fallen off the makeshift swing
   Oh, hosh hosh   at the back of the flats. A
                                          couple of young English
                                          children from the flat downstairs
                                          comforted him*)

   We don't mean to cry do we
   No
   That's right
   O yeh you do
   I'm happy now   (*Here after only a few weeks in
(*indistinct sounds*)   London, he does a creditable
                                          imitation of the English
                                          accent — 'hosh' equals 'hush'*)

We have a swing
O pee doodle
Fell off the swing   (*tune of Humpty Dumpty*)
. . . clumsy
Why you cryning, don't cry, hosh don't prosh will
you don't cry
Going to have a little drop . . .

Dumpy, dumpy dip　　　　　　　*(continues humming in this vein)*
Look . . . my handle
Now got lot . . . two handles
Wash it
He has enough
had enough
(indistinct sounds)
　Night time　　　　　*(simulated sleep sounds and humming)*
　Shopping bag, shopping bag, shopping bag *(chanted)*
　Up the dee, up the dee, up the dee
　Woo b doo　　　　*(to the tune of 'London Bridge is falling down')*
(1 minute silence, then extended humming)
　Go to sleep now　　　　　　　　*(simulated snoring)*
　Night time
(laughing)
　Hallo, hallo
(laughing)

　Der, der, der, der
　The fire'n, the fire'n, the fire fire
　The feer, feer, feer　　　　　*(to the tune of 'The Farmer
　　　　　　　　　　　　　　　　　　in the Dell')*
　The fire, fire, fire
　The fire, fire, fire, fire, fire　　*(On our first day in London we
　　. . . engine　　　　　　　　took up lodgings in a poky room
　The fire engine　　　　　　　in a hotel in Gower Street.
　It boom boom　　　　　　　The traffic was loud. The kids
　Fire engine　　　　　　　　rushed to the window in amaze-
　It boom boom　　　　　　　ment when a fire engine went
　Fire engine　　　　　　　　past at full blast. Simon
　I broom, broom, broom　　　was really impressed by the
　The fire's out *(glissando)*　　'different' sound.)*
　The fire's out, the fire's out *(sharp repetition)*
　The fire's out *(glissando)*
　The fire's out *(repeated more softly)*
　The fire's out *(still more softly)*
　The fire's out *(louder)*
　The fire's out, the fire's out *(sharp repetition)*
　Fire's out *(glissando)*
　The fire's out, the fire's out
　Fire's out *(glissando)*
　The fire's out *(echo effect)*
　Fire . . . is *(pauses)*
　Engine, engine

(*indistinct sounds; grunting*)
    It's night time
    It's night time (*chanted*)
    The fire's out, the fire's out, the fire's out, the fire's out
    The fire's in, the fire's out (*repeated*)
    The fire's out, the fire's in
    The fire's in
    Der, der, der, der, der (*simulated siren*)
    Din, din, din, din
    The children go to the bicycles
    . . . bikes
    See the scratch there
    Bang, bang
    Bzz, Bzz, Bzzzzz
    Trr . . rouble makers (*swatting sounds*)
    Stupid
    Two kisses
    Two kisses
    One kiss, another little kiss, another little kiss
(*hums a tune from 'Gilligan's Island' — a television programme — occasional words recognizable*)
    He's got two . . . (*simulated snoring*)

    Teddy bear
    Stop crying
    Stop crying
    Bassandra
    Bassandra Boomer, Bassandra Boomer, Bassandra
    Bassandra Boomer (*chanting*)

> (*Cassandra is the name of the daughter of a Malay couple living in the same block of flats*)

    Bassandra Jean
    We don't know what to do
    We don't know what to do
    Burp durp du durp du (*'Pop Goes the Weasel'*)
(*nonsense sounds to the same tume — the sound mmm — predominates; finishes with . . .*)
    . . . cover you up
    Uppy uppy yp yp
    I'm dead

12   THE SPITTING IMAGE

    Ition box   (*idiot box*)
    What's on the ition box old boy
(*indistinct sounds*)
    A soldier
    Am I dead
    It's hot
    Hallo Caffy, Caffy
    Caffrine, Caffrin (*to sleeping sister*)
(*Yawn*)
    Night Caffrine
(*ten second pause*)
    I told you . . .
    A piggy nick
    A piggy back
    A piggy back on me
    Right under there (chanting)
    Right under here on my head
    I don't know what to do
    I don't know what to do
    I can't put her head
    I don't know what to do
    Pat her
(*indistinct sounds*)
    Oh, no you can't
    Oh, yes I can
(*repeated three times*)
    Oh, yes I can
    Oh, no I'm not
(*repeated three times*)
    That's the slip
    It is the slip to go in the water   (*Friends back in Australia*
                                                                                        had a swimming pool with a
    That's the water down there   *slippery dip*)
    and you jump
    jumpy, jumpy, jumpy (*chant*)
    We had a piggy
    A piggy nick
(*sound like R, rrr . . .*)
    A piggy nick
    A piggy nick?
    Oh, that's another good word
    Squash in
(*indistinct sounds*)

I don't know what to do
A dear, dear, dear
A dear, dear, dear (*repeated chanting*)
. . .
A dear, a dear a do ya, you do, you do,
you do ya
(*1½ minute silence, then simulated sleep sounds*)
   Uncle Grant had a . . .   (*Uncle Grant, back in Australia,*
   Car, car   *had various nicknames for*
   (*simulated sleep sounds — yawns*)   *Simon, including, "Car, car"*)
   Why did you turn it back there?

Catherine, I love you
(*fifteen second silence*)
Ready to go
Fireman. Fireman. The Fireman
Bzz Bzz Bzz
Wee wee wee wee wee its
Is it a plane, is it a bird   (*Obviously from the old favourite*
No No it's . . . aeroplane   *Is it a bird? Is it a plane?*
Is it a bird, is it a plane   *No it's Superman!*)
It's a teddy bear
It's a upside teddy bear
Goldilocks, goldilocks (*practised to become something like "bawdy-looks"*)

Leven, twelve, thirty, forty, fifty, sixty, seventy,
eighty, ninety, seventy, eighty, ninety

Make a big moo
Muckety, muckety, muckety, muck, mucky, mucky, mucky, muck

The mouse went down, up and down . . . (*pause*)
Jiggety, jiggety, jock

Catherine where's your Humphrey   (*her bear*)

The mouse went down (*to a tune*)
Jiggety, jiggety, jock
. . . ran up the clock
The mouse went down (*increased tempo for this line*)
Jiggety, jiggety, jock (*slower*)
(*This sequence repeated three times*)
   . . . Gosh you ran down
The mouse ran up the clock
The mouse went down,

Jiggety, jiggety, jock
The mouse went up again (*no time*)
The mouse ran up the clock
The mouse ran down
Jiggety, jiggety, jock
I got an . . .
The mouse ran up the clock
(*eight second silence; humming, one minute silence*)
And we couldn't see the light out of that door
did we?   (*The kids always liked to be*
Didn't like it shut   *able to see a light on at night*)
The we didn't see the light in the light bulb did we? No we didn't.
I can't get under my step
And I . . .
I'n Johnny
Big ladies and boys
Look at me I'n Johnny
Mnm Mnm Mnm . . . (*continued*)
Robert doody, Roberty doody   (*'Doody' was the name for his*
Mnm   *penis. His daddy's first*
Cutthroat Jake   *name is Robert*)
We just about ready
Cutthroat Jake
We just about ready   (*from Captain Pugwash*)
Cutthroat Jake
Just about ready to fight
Hush throw sh . . . ready to go
In the post office
The post office, the post office, the post   (*Mummy had taken them to*
office (*rising intonation*)   *the post office that day*)
Ready to go
Now I don't know what to do
Oh no, no no no
I don't know what to do ee dee dot   (*all this to "Pop Goes the*
Pip pit de dit dare   *Weasel"*)
Mee-oo me-oo me-ooo me-ooo
And the aeroplane goes d da d   (*Simon was intrigued and a little*
I'n locked in   *overwhelmed by the Jumbo jet*
Mnm   *which brought us to London.*
I'n yucking to him   *He asked how you could get back*
Big yucky, I've been   *down to earth if you wanted to.*)
I can't reach
How could we get down?
(*indistinct sentence*)

Off to the wood or the blocks or the (*Close to our flat there was*
wood or the blocks or the wood or the *a pleasant wooded reserve*)
blocks or the blocks or the blocks. Box
order box order box forty dorty dorter
dox (*rhythmical*)
(*hums "Pop Goes the Weasel"*)
(*two minutes silence; indistinct muttering*)
   Catherine put your head up
   I like it better up
(*eight second silence*)
   I don't know what to do ooo oo oo   (*"Pop Goes the Weasel"*)
(*2½ minutes silence; whispering; 2½ minutes silence*)
(*yawn*)
(*1½ minutes silence*)
   I don't known what to do
(*indistinct noises; "mnm" predominant*)
   Wrap him up, wrap in up, wrapn up
   Rapnuptum, rapnuptum, rapnuptum, mnm, mnm
(*one minute silence*)
   I see wacko, wackee, wacko, wackee
   wackee, wackee, wackee, co eee coo eee coo eee
   And we have a runda bock
   We have a lovely box
   We have a lovely run a run
   . . . a runny fun
   . . . Over the cowshed (*breaking into the song "K-K-K-Katie"*)
   I'll be . . . (*indistinct*)
   Waiting at the g, g, g, g, g train   (*A song he had taken a fancy to*
   Over the cowshed   *back in Australia. I think*
   I'll be waiting at the   *Grumpy used to sing it to him*)
   g,g, g, g, g, kitchen door
   Skippy, Skippy   (*His favourite Australian*
   Skippy the nice kangaroo   *television programme had been*
   D, d, d, doo   *"Skippy, The Bush Kangaroo"*)
   Der, de der de der (*tune of "Skippy" which
   flows into another television signature tune*)

   Sh
(*mumbling*)
   Nice comfortable isn't it
(*indistinct sounds*)
   Wakin you up
   That's clever
   I can knee up

Oh time to get up
No it's time to go to sleep
When I go . . .

Ring ding ling
Time to get up
Tired
(*mumbling*)
They're pushing me down aren't they?   (*I can't resist drawing attention to the symbolism*)
(*two minute silence; yawn; indistinct sounds*)
Sing . . . yella
the ella sumporine (*sings*)
We all live in the ella sumporine (*To the tune of We All Live in A Yellow Submarine*)
ella sumporine the ella sumporine
We all live in the ella sum . . .
(*and the rest is silence*)

Simon, taking on patterns of experience and soothing words like ballast, finally dives into the sub-conscious of sleep. We all live in a yellow submarine. We need to lay the ghosts and demons of each day before sleep washes over us. What can I say about Simon's amazing method of rocking his own cradle?

Three years ago, inspired by the late Ruth Weir's study of the monologues of her son, Anthony, I mined my transcript with a scholar's zeal, doing word counts and analyses of the metalinguisitic practice of vowels and consonants. I noted the way in which he built up phrases progressively; how he punned and rhymed and played and associated and dramatized; how he tenaciously worked to reconcile Australia and England.

In seminars at the Institute of Education I used Simon to illustrate the theories of Chomsky and Jimmy Britton (Simon, in the spectator role) and Jean Piaget and Lev Semenovitch Vygotsky. I used him to "prove" that we all have a have a natural urge to tell stories and write poems and compose songs. Now I can't bring myself to repeat the linguistic dissections. I just want to show.

Look on his work you teachers and despair. Despair because you cannot teach him more than the merest fraction of what he teaches himself about language and life. Relax and enjoy your children and enjoy yourselves.

It's all a question of floral arrangement   3
or
How to fail school on day one!

Wearing the Right Clothes

Whenever you open your mouth, you give yourself away to somebody. Every utterance you make provides your audience with classificatory material about you—your relationship to the group, to an individual within it, your membership or non membership. The language you use allows your audience to "slot" you in and make sense of you. How you "measure up" to your audience may cause you to be elevated or it may promote a slight frown or some other act which registers distaste.

Have you ever experienced the embarrassment of arriving at a social function to find yourself inappropriately dressed? In such a situation, you are at least left with the comfortable knowledge that you can readily exchange the clothes that you are wearing with others at home which would indeed be "proper" for the occasion. It is slightly more complex (though no less embarrassing) if you find that you are not "talking right". When this happens you immediately reveal yourself as an outsider—and there is not the same reassurance that you can just go home and change!

Language is a more powerful social determiner than is clothing because it is so interwoven with identity. When a child learns his language he also learns his culture[1] and his relationships to the world around him. The language of an individual reflects his culture and his culture finds expression in his language; the two factors, language and culture, are inextricably linked. All normal individuals have both language and culture which act as a filter between themselves and the outside world. When they speak, their audience registers both that language and culture to place the speaker in relation to the audience. Such relationships involve hierarchical judgments.

"Haves" and "Have-nots"

Because of the information about cultural background which is revealed through language, language acts as an agent of social control.[2] Language is a means of keeping people in their place. It separates the "haves" from the "have-nots" and maintains a stratified order. Through their language employers remind employees of their relationship; parents demonstrate to children; males to females; teachers to pupils; public servants to the public. Each speech fellowship group[3] has its own codes and rituals which serve to discriminate the members of the group from the non-members. The power structure is revealed when you don't "talk right" within a particular group.

> "Because people who rarely talk together will talk differently, differences in speech tell what groups a man belongs to. He uses them to claim and proclaim his identity, and society uses them to keep him under control. The person who talks right as we do is one of us. The person who talks wrong is an outsider, strange and suspicious and we must make him inferior if we can. That is one purpose of education. In a school system run like ours, by white business men, instruction in the mother tongue includes formal initiation into the linguistic prejudices of the middle class."[4]

This elaborate code which detects those who don't talk right, has been termed "linguistic table manners".[5] It is like using the wrong fork. The food had no less nutritional value and there is no difference in taste — but everyone knows that you are not a member of the group. Linguistic table manners have nothing to do with the quality of communication; they are of social value only! [6]

Table Manners in the Classroom

The school has evolved its own codes and they reflect the linguistic and cultural backgrounds of the teachers. They are the table manners of those who have had a successful career in schools and are codes which are primarily the monopoly of the middle class. This is very convenient if all the students in the school happen to be middle-class. But, unfortunately, many of them are not.

Many children arrive at school with linguistic table manners which the teacher may find distasteful. It is these table manners which the teacher uses to determine the relationship of the child to the school in general, to the class and to the teacher himself. The language of some children will help them to claim membership to the same group as that of the teacher. Conversely, there will be other children who clearly demonstrate their distance from such a group. They don't talk right, and from their first day at school, they are outsiders.

Within the school, there is positive value placed on educational attainment, and educational attainment demands that activities be performed in a certain way. The school declares that *only* certain language forms and certain experiences are valid for educational purposes. It is a valid experience to see the school as an agent of upward social mobility. It is valid to seek to do well in school in order to get a good job. It is invalid to persist with linguistic forms such as "Yous", "we seen" and "we done" (despite the fact that, linguistically, these are perfectly acceptable forms). It is invalid to be exempt from the meritocracy and competition. To succeed in school, it is necessary to master the school's linguistic table manners, and this is a most difficult exercise. It is certainly beyond the capacity of most children just entering school.

Obviously, many children come to school without the linguistic and cultural forms which the school requires for the purposes of education.

As those who have profited from the diet which the school offers, teachers tend to act as custodians, ensuring that the values remain uncontaminated. Most teachers are by definition "experts" in what constitutes "correct" linguistic and cultural forms for education. They value the linguistic and cultural forms which they possess and which have enabled them to achieve in an educational institution. Too many teachers do not value those linguistic and cultural forms which are not their own and which they classify as inadequate for school learning. Children who do not meet these requirements are educational failures.

> "In our culture 'failure' in educational terms is failure from a strictly middle-class point of view . . .'failure in the eleven plus' . . . 'failure to gain a place at Oxford or Cambridge' or lower down the middle-class, 'failure to find a secure and well paid middle-class career.'"[7]

For those children who do not happen to share the linguistic and cultural forms of the school, there is an obstacle. Their experiences, their identity, in extreme cases, could be classified as non-existent. A headmistress, addressing new members of staff, stated the following.

> "I feel it is only reasonable to be quite frank with you concerning the nature of the children we have here. You must realize that this is a very deprived area with a high proportion of immigrant children. These children come to school with no cultural background from homes where there is often no reading matter, little discipline and few social values. We have to provide them with culture and imagination."[8]

To be more accurate, what the headmistress should be saying is that these children have no middle-class reading matter, no middle-class discipline and no middle-class social values. It is the task of the school to provide them with middle-class culture and middle-class imagination which is consistent with her own. She is saying that these children are different from her, and that is an accurate assessment, but she is also stating they are deficient (or devoid), and that is an unenlightened and ill-informed value judgment.

Elitist Parameters

The assumption behind the headmistress' address is that only certain linguistic and cultural forms are allowed for education, and they are the forms which she and her fellow teachers have at their disposal. She does not question the legitimacy of her evaluation.

An elitist view of culture and of formal learning works against those children whose origins place them outside the elitist parameters. Is it that school failure is simply a measure of those children who fail to be middle-class? Are children being asked on their first day either to conform or to fail? Are the experiences, imaginings, language and culture of some children being misinterpreted?

Unfortunately, many young teachers who enter the classroom are convinced of the validity of their own educational experience, assured of the positive value of climbing the educational ladder, and are inspired to bring these values to their students and guide them on the golden path to success. Such a framework may preclude them from seeing the value of the children's own experience and there is room for misunderstanding when the children do not see the teacher as the bearer of great gifts.

When school failure equals cultural failure, and when children may fail to meet the linguistic and cultural values of their teachers on the first day, then the school has created its own monster. Children who fail from the beginning have this expectation transmitted to them and it should not be surprising if they proceed to fulfil the expectation and conform to the failure syndrome as they progress through the school.

Floral Arrangements

Middle-class values prevail in the school. Middle-class children succeed in school. There has been suggestion that those children who are not middle-class are disadvantaged. So they are. The school does not find them legitimate pupils. If schools were to reflect the values of Aborigines, or migrants, or women, or dockworkers then those who were not Aboriginal, migrant, female or dockworkers would also be disadvantaged. They could be classified as school failures.

It is a form of arrogance (not supported by anthropology) to suggest that the cultural experiences of one group are superior to those of another. Yet it would appear that this is an assumption within the school. It is all a matter of floral arrangements. Though they both serve the same decorative purpose everyone knows that dried floral arrangements are infinitely superior to plastic flowers. If you are a plastic flower at the school gate, then you will be a failure until you learn that dried floral arrangements are the only legitimate means for successful home decorating.

Notes

1. Rosen, Harold. *Language and Class*. Falling Wall Press, U.K. 1962.
2. Flower, F. "The Language of Failure" in *English in Education*. 4(3), 1970.
3. Mackay, David. "Language standards and attitudes: a response", in Marchwardt, A. H. (ed), *Language and Language Learning*. N.C.T.E., Illinois, 1968.
4. Sledd, James. "Bidialectalism: the Linguistics of White Supremacy", in Hipple, T. W. (ed), *Readings for Teaching English in Secondary Schools*. Macmillan, New York, 1973, p. 265.
5. Creber, Patrick, W. *Lost for Words*. Penguin, 1973.
6. Hamp, Eric P. "Language in a Few Words: With Notes on a Rereading 1966", in DeCecco, J. (ed), *The Psychology of Language Thought and Instruction*. Holt, Rinehart and Winston, London, 1969.
7. Duane, Michael, "Speech and Reading: The Language of Failure", in *English in Education*, 4(3), 1970, p. 63.
8. Dawson, L. "Advice from the Head", in *Teaching London Kids*. L.A.T.E., n.d.

4 More guesses equals freedom

Correction Codes

Once upon a time there were very simple rules for playing the school writing game. You started at the beginning of the year with the first page of your composition book, and you wrote out all the rules. You set out the composition correction code in your best writing.

    Composition Correction Code
    Sp— Spelling error
    G — Grammatical error
    P — Punctuation error
    /P— New paragraph required
    S — Sentence construction error
    ∧ — Word left out
    — — Poor expression

You took great pride in the neatness of your work as you wrote out the code. The teacher carefully explained all the rules and showed you how you made your corrections when you got an Sp or a G written in red on your composition. Everyone knew about correctness and corrections.

For the second lesson, after you had taken a new page, ruled your margin and put the date, you were given a title. They were nice, comfortable titles that you didn't have to think too much about; you know the ones—"A day at the beach"; "The road toll"; "A narrow escape"; "The day the school bus didn't come". The teacher gave you forty minutes, without talking, to write about one and a half pages, according to the rules.

Then it was collected, and you waited with bated breath for the following week when you would get it back. This lesson was called "Follow up" and your main concern was how many rules you had broken. The more rules you broke, the less marks you got and the more corrections you had to make. This was an easy lesson.

MORE GUESSES EQUALS FREEDOM   23

Life was pretty simple in those days. Not like it is today. I don't really know why it all changed, but evidently those in the know decided that there was something wrong with composition correction codes and the teachers became obsessed about creative writing.

Today we have teachers who keep smiling and say there aren't any rules any more. And you are a bit in the dark when you don't know the rules of the game. Don't they realize how difficult they are making it? How can you ever start to write when you don't know what they want? There's a lot of pressure when you just have to keep guessing all the time.

Guessing Correctly

This is a typical day—Tuesday is not just composition day any more. The teacher comes in and says:
"Well, what would you like to do today?"
Now you all know he has got something in particular in mind, but you've all got to try and guess what it is. It's not as if he really wants to know what we want to do today. I mean, I know how it would go down if we all said—"Go outside" or "Have a sleep", so they are not real guesses.
No, by now you have a fair idea of what the answer is that he wants.

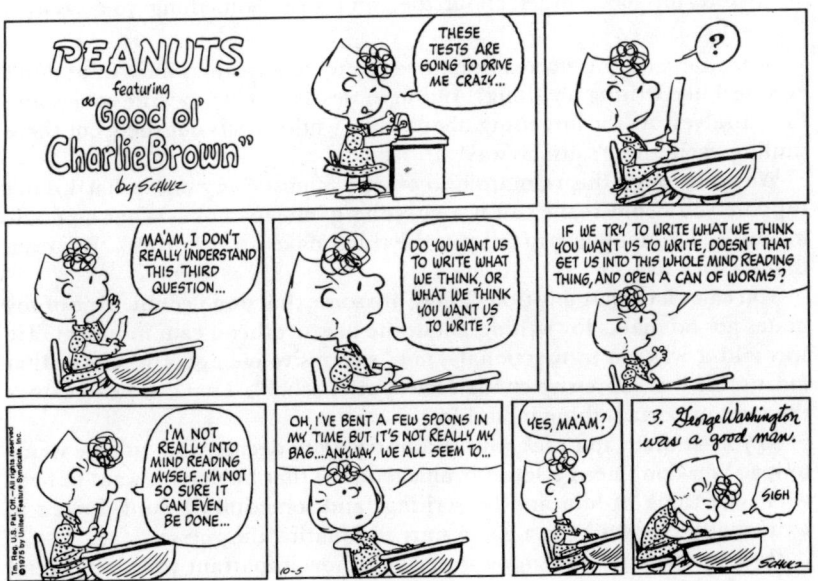

There are about three standard replies guaranteed to turn him on:
- We'd all *love* to *write* something!
- Could we *please* read our *novels*?
- Can we do *creative drama*?

Now one of these is sure to make his day, but you are not allowed to come out with it straight away. You have to hedge around for a while. So we throw in a half-hearted "Listen to a Shakespearean record" or "Watch a video-tape." You mustn't be too eager about these, because he gets quite put out.

But then, with great enthusiasm, we bring on one of the answers he is looking for. That's when the lesson starts. And the sure success guess is "Can we please write something?" He's always relieved when we get to it.

So that part is all right really. I mean there's no great puzzle about it. You've got to admit we've got it down to a routine performance. The real trouble starts when we actually come to writing something. I mean, what do you write?

Someone always starts the ball rolling with "O.K. sir, what will we write?" and that's the cue for his performance. It goes something like this:

> "Oh, I don't want to tell you what to write. You think of something for yourself. I don't want to be a dictator. It wouldn't be the same if you wrote for me. Forget about me, and write something you *need* to write."

Now where do you start. I don't *need* to write anything, most of us don't even feel like writing anything. And here we are having to write something for ourselves. As for forgetting about him, while he sits out the front there smiling, well, there's just no way!

We go through this rigmarole so often—almost every day—that I don't suppose you could really call it a guessing game anymore. What he really means is "I'm not going to tell you the title, make up your own". But even that's a trick too.

You can't have just any title. There are some that don't count. One of my mates got no marks for writing about the new overhead cam in his car. He was told it was too transactional—not "expressive enough", whatever that means. He was expressive enough later, after school. That overhead cam is the most important thing in his life.

So you sit there and rack your brains trying to decide what title he wants today. You don't need a lot of brains to know that he doesn't want to hear what you think of him and his writing (and sometimes I think I *need* to write that!). No, you've just got to start eliminating the guesses.

Does he want all that soppy stuff about how important your best friend is—or does he want something with "guts" which means you have to say a few nasty things and throw in some swear words for sincerity?

Well, this is where you have to take a punt. I used to think that you could go one way or the other because he didn't seem to give you any clues to help you decide. But I've been wondering about it a bit lately, because when we compare notes later, we all seem to have guessed the same way. I mean we all seem to write about either our loving mothers or our hateful fathers. It's almost enough to have you believing in E.S.P.

But the fun doesn't stop here. You are still only about half way there once you've got your title. Guess number two is, *how* does he want you to say it today? Someone always has to be the guinea pig and ask.

"Please sir, should I just let myself go and become involved in my writing, or should I consider that this is for assessment?"

Translated, for those of you who aren't really up on the game, this means do I have to do all that no punctuation jazz or can I go back to the good old rules? You know, I don't think he really knows which one he wants most of the time. Anyhow, the answer is a trap, and you have to be careful.

"I don't want to limit you in anyway. I'm only interested in your *genuine communication*."

Now this won't help at all. Some days *genuine* means that he doesn't want punctuation, and other days *communication* means you can't make sense without it. If you jump the wrong way and make an effort to leave out the full stops, he can tell you he can't make sense of it. And if you leave them in, he can say it's artificial, you didn't get "immersed" in it. So it's hard to win on this one.

Assessment

And then of course, there's the mark! Sometimes we all get going and really make an effort, and then when we've finished, he says it would spoil it if he marked it. I mean, what does he think he's doing to us? All that effort wasted. But if that's not enough, sometimes he gets quite sneaky.

There are days when he speaks softly and tells us we are not to be threatened in any way. He says to write just the things that come into your head. Well not much comes into my head unless I try very hard. So I just sit there and have a bit of a snooze, and think about some of the things that happened during the day. I do a few jottings, just so he knows I was there — and then blow me down, if he doesn't collect it and say its for assessment! And I haven't even tried to get a mark.

Now that's when he goes a bit too far. What chance have you got when he pulls stunts like that? And he doesn't give you a second chance, you know.

Sometimes when I haven't made the right guesses — and I ask him can I do it again, now I know what he wants, he gets all upset. You may find out he wanted something soppy and you wrote something nasty, or today was "no punctuation day" and you put in full stops, or you thought it was to fill in the lesson and now he's going to give you a mark. You ask for another chance at the game, and he says it is not genuine communication. He says it's artificial to want to rewrite it. And he thinks he is being frustrated!

Every time he comes into the classroom I think "Here we go again, what do we have to find out today?" But he seems happy enough most of the time. Come to think of it, he sounded very proud when I heard him talking to another teacher the other day. He was saying what a spontaneous class this is and how he gives us all the freedom in the world. Now I'll have to guess what spontaneous and freedom mean. I wonder what they'll add to the probability of getting the right guess.

Good grade three sentences and a joining word   5

Daddy	Tell me about your writing at school — your compositions.
Catherine (aged seven)	Oh, well you see, we write these compositions and we get points for these compositions. We've done one about a lost child, one about a teddy bear and I forget the other one but my highest mark yet is nine.
D	What do you mean by a mark, what's that?
C	Marks, you see, ten out of ten or nine out of ten. Sometimes you get 7½.
D	Has anyone got ten?
C	Yes. Some children have.
D	Have they?
C	Mm.
D	What do you have to do to get ten?
C	Not make any mistakes, not turn around and talk to anybody and you're not allowed to talk at all.
D	I see. Why aren't you allowed to talk?
C	If you talk you get half a mark taken off.
D	Why?
C	Because you make somebody else do a mistake.
D	How much do you write?
C	Oo, about two pages full.
D	Do you? Where do you get all the words from? To write two pages?
C	We just make it up.

D	How long do you get to write?
C	Oo, about from morning recess to afternoon recess.
D	You get a long, long time, do you?
C	Mm.
D	Do you all write on the same thing?
C	Yes. When we write about a teddy bear we all write about a teddy bear. When we write about a lost child then we all write about a lost child.
D	Do you do something before you write? Do you talk about what you might say?
C	Yes. But um, on lost, on the lost page, well, um, you see, we had to write it all down on, on a paper and then write it into our books.
D	What do you mean you had to write it down on paper? Everyone wrote it down on paper?
C	Yes.
D	What? The same thing or their own story or what?
C	Their own story on a piece of paper and then they had to copy it into their books.
D	Oh yes? Why do you do that? So that it looks better?
C	No, because you've got to get it all right—make all the sentences right.
D	What's a sentence? (*long pause*)
C	Mm, a couple of words.
D	Oh, I see.
D	Do you talk about the bear or lost and does Miss what's her name?
C	Mrs. X.
D	Yes, what does she do to help you?
C	We put our hands up and she says always start it off with: "I am a teddy bear and my name is so and so."
D	She tells you how to start off each piece does she?
C	Mm.
D	Do you do that?
C	Yes. She writes some good beginning sentences on the board but we don't have to use those.
D	They're just there to help you?

C	Mm. You can use them all if you like.
D	And which is the one you got 9/10 for?
C	Um. Lost, and another one.
D	And do you think that they were your best?
C	My Birthday and Lost.
D	Do you think they were your best compositions? (*Pause*) Were some of your others just as good?
C	Mm.
D	Why did you lose your marks then? Why didn't you get 10/10?
C	Because um, you see, we put um long sentences that were too long.
D	You put sentences that were too long?
C	Mm. If you forget to do capitals or full stops you get a mark taken off.
D	Would you like to write some of your own stories rather than the ones she tells you to write? I mean what about that nice lion story that you wrote? Do you remember, when that party was on here?
C	Mm.
D	Do you do any stories like that of your own at school? Where she says you can go away and write something of your own if you like? Does she do that at all?
C	No.
D	You're not allowed to write your own stuff?
C	No. Not in our composition book.
D	Well, but can you write it in other places if you want to?
C	Yes, you can do it in busy work but there's no busy work paper.
D	So you can't really do writing in busy work?
C	No.
D	Oh. Would you write better stories, longer stories if you were on your own do you think?
C	Mm.
D	What sort of things would you like to write about?
C	Animals.
D	What? Fairy stories or stories about . . .

C	Fairy stories.
Mummy	She likes stories about animals — like the lions, and (what was it?), the kangaroo and peacock....
D	Mm. Do you ever write sort of poetry stuff?
C	Oh. Yes, we have a poetry book but we don't do very many poems. We did one about: "I think mice are rather nice."
D	What, you mean the teacher read it to you?
C	Mm. Then she puts it down on the board and we have to copy it into our books.
D	Oh. You don't write poems of your own about things?
C	No.
D	Oh. Well what do you think is the best time in school?
C	Um, dictation.
D	Oh. Why do you like that?
C	Because you see, she reads it out to you in little words and sometimes she only gives you one word at a time and you get marks for it.
D	Yes.
C	And you get a "very good" stamp or "for progress" stamp.
D	And why do you like it? Do you get satisfaction out of it? In some way? What do you like about it?
C	You get marks.
D	Do you get good marks?
C	Mm.
D	What sort of marks do you get for that?
C	Ten out of ten . . . or something.
D	I see. What's the difference, main difference, between the infant and primary school?
C	'Cause you have lunch inside and when you have assembly you don't go into the big room, you just go out in the yard and you just stand up, you don't sing or anything, you just say a couple of words.
D	Yes, what else is different inside when you're doing your lessons?
C	Um?
D	Do you think back to what it was like last year and compare it with this year?

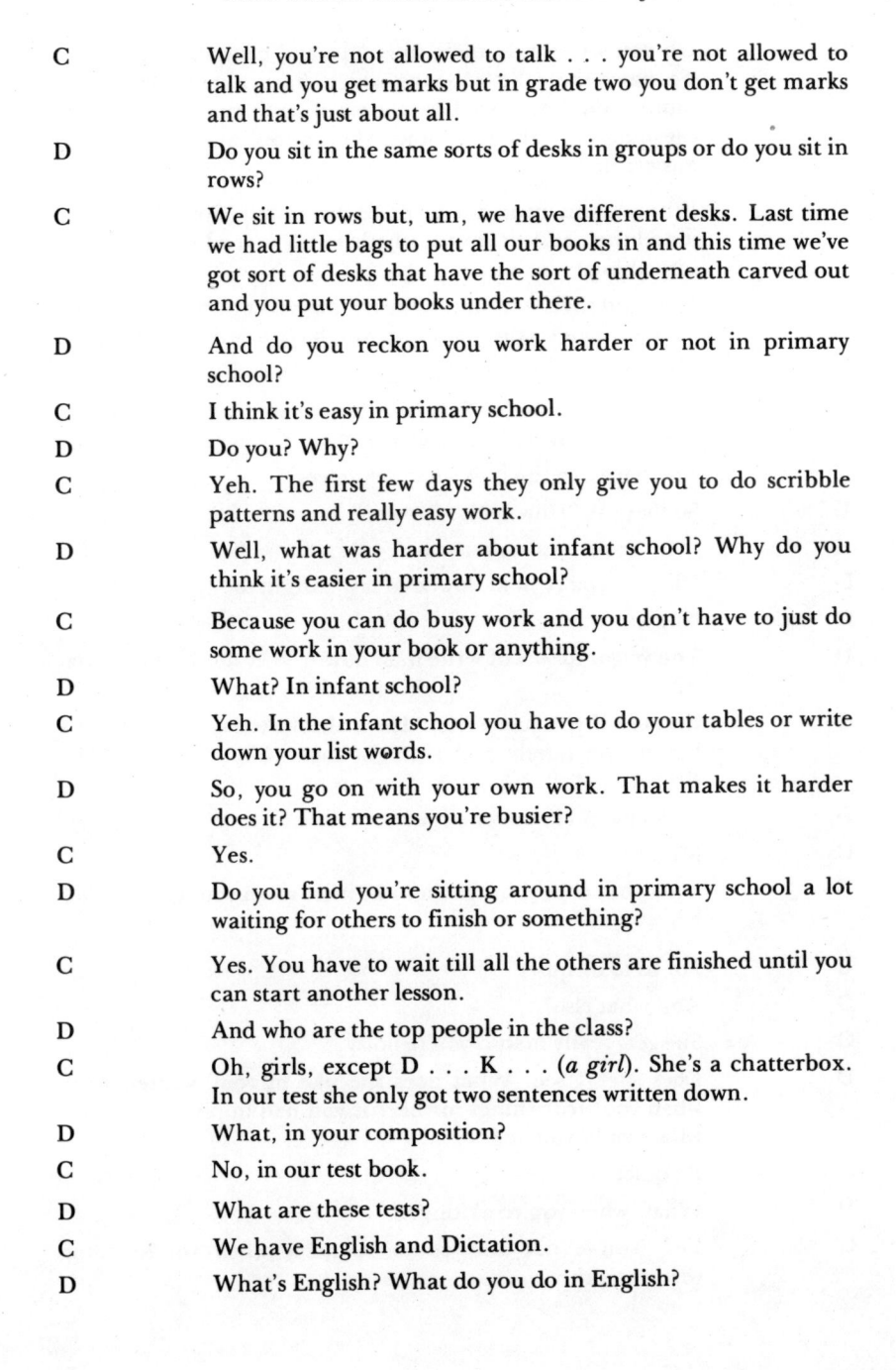

C	Well, you're not allowed to talk . . . you're not allowed to talk and you get marks but in grade two you don't get marks and that's just about all.
D	Do you sit in the same sorts of desks in groups or do you sit in rows?
C	We sit in rows but, um, we have different desks. Last time we had little bags to put all our books in and this time we've got sort of desks that have the sort of underneath carved out and you put your books under there.
D	And do you reckon you work harder or not in primary school?
C	I think it's easy in primary school.
D	Do you? Why?
C	Yeh. The first few days they only give you to do scribble patterns and really easy work.
D	Well, what was harder about infant school? Why do you think it's easier in primary school?
C	Because you can do busy work and you don't have to just do some work in your book or anything.
D	What? In infant school?
C	Yeh. In the infant school you have to do your tables or write down your list words.
D	So, you go on with your own work. That makes it harder does it? That means you're busier?
C	Yes.
D	Do you find you're sitting around in primary school a lot waiting for others to finish or something?
C	Yes. You have to wait till all the others are finished until you can start another lesson.
D	And who are the top people in the class?
C	Oh, girls, except D . . . K . . . (*a girl*). She's a chatterbox. In our test she only got two sentences written down.
D	What, in your composition?
C	No, in our test book.
D	What are these tests?
C	We have English and Dictation.
D	What's English? What do you do in English?

C	Oh you see, we do these full stops and capitals and you see we have these little books which have about the Brown family and they have these couple of sentences and they have the questions about it down the bottom and you have to answer them.
D	What do you mean about the Brown family? Sort of you read it and then answer, to see whether you've read it properly or something?
C	Yeh, and then you, um, write the answers down in sentences. You just can't write the word, you have to write it down in a sentence.
D	What do you mean? Can you give me an example? What do you mean you can't use a word?
C	You have to write it down in sentences.
D	So they say "How is Mr. Brown?" . . .
C	"Mr. Brown is alright today."
D	Oh . . . You're not allowed to say "alright today."
C	No.
D	You've got to sort of write it all down. Why do you think that is?
C	Because if you just write, "He is alright today", they have a boy in the family and it might mean him. You say "Mr. Brown . . ."
D	To show you know who it is?
C	Mm.
D	And what does your teacher like most when you do things for her?
C	For us to be quiet.
D	And what else?
C	She gets really mad if you're noisy.
D	Does she? I see. What does she like in your written work when you write things for her? If you had to please her most what would you do?
C	Be quiet.
D	What, when you're writing?
C	Yes. You're not allowed to be noisy when you're doing written work.

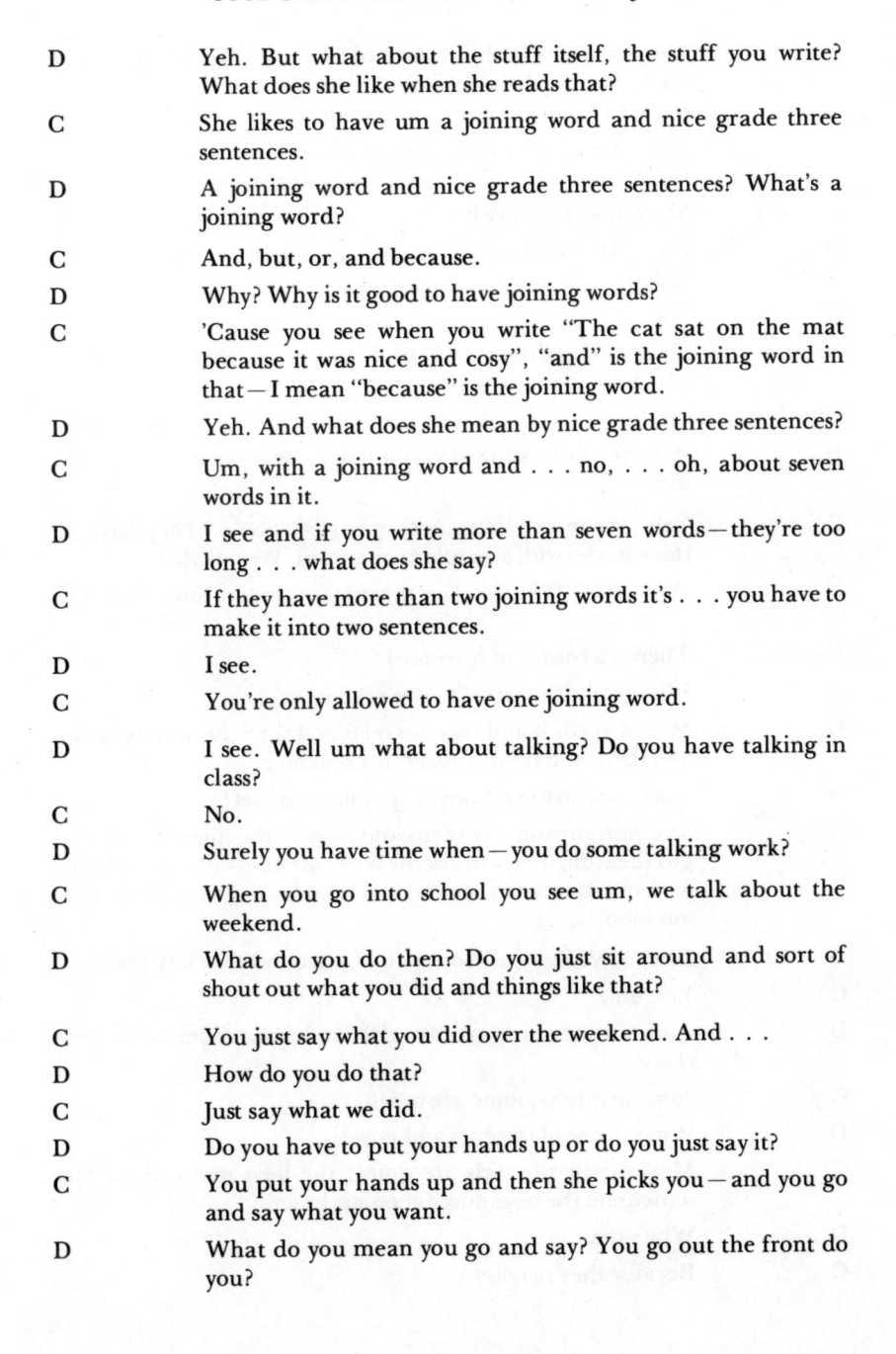

GOOD GRADE THREE SENTENCES AND A JOINING WORD   33

D   Yeh. But what about the stuff itself, the stuff you write? What does she like when she reads that?

C   She likes to have um a joining word and nice grade three sentences.

D   A joining word and nice grade three sentences? What's a joining word?

C   And, but, or, and because.

D   Why? Why is it good to have joining words?

C   'Cause you see when you write "The cat sat on the mat because it was nice and cosy", "and" is the joining word in that — I mean "because" is the joining word.

D   Yeh. And what does she mean by nice grade three sentences?

C   Um, with a joining word and . . . no, . . . oh, about seven words in it.

D   I see and if you write more than seven words — they're too long . . . what does she say?

C   If they have more than two joining words it's . . . you have to make it into two sentences.

D   I see.

C   You're only allowed to have one joining word.

D   I see. Well um what about talking? Do you have talking in class?

C   No.

D   Surely you have time when — you do some talking work?

C   When you go into school you see um, we talk about the weekend.

D   What do you do then? Do you just sit around and sort of shout out what you did and things like that?

C   You just say what you did over the weekend. And . . .

D   How do you do that?

C   Just say what we did.

D   Do you have to put your hands up or do you just say it?

C   You put your hands up and then she picks you — and you go and say what you want.

D   What do you mean you go and say? You go out the front do you?

C Yeh, you go out the front and you say "Mrs. X, girls and boys, during the weekend, I went to a barbecue, and we played a couple of games and went home."

D I see. And then what happens? Does she tell you how to say it better or do you just—does she just let you say it?

C She just lets you say it.

D I see. And do the children ask you questions about what you did?

C No.

D Or anything like that? They don't say, "Catherine, what did you do?"

C No.

D Are they interesting? Do you like to hear what other people did?

C Yeh. We've got these Active English books. They have all these stories with a couple of questions. We talk then.

D What sort? What do you mean? You read a story and then . . .

C There's a couple of questions.

D Who reads the story? Do you read it or . . .

C Mrs. X reads it and then we read and then she asks questions and then we have to answer in a sentence.

D What, not writing down . . . just on your feet?

C You just put your hand up and answer the question. If it's a girl then, oh, then you ask the next question—the girl asks the next question and then the boy answers and he asks the next question.

D I see. So you go girl, boy, girl, boy around the classroom.

C Yes, um.

D And tell me, how are the girls and boys different in your class?

C Some are noisy, some are quiet.

D What, some of the girls and boys?

C Mm, mostly the girls are quiet; the boys muck about and sometimes the boys miss out on art lesson.

D Why's that?

C Because they're noisy.

D	Um. What do you think is the best . . . Sorry, what were you going to say?
C	They miss out on art lesson and they . . . Mrs. X says that if they keep on making noise they'll have to stay in after school and have a lesson on how to change lessons being quiet.
D	Have they ever done that? Have they ever been kept in?
C	No. But she says they will the next time.
D	What about . . . Does Mrs. X hit children? Or not?
C	Yes. When she's really mad she does. She doesn't hit girls.
D	Oh. Well what does she do when she hits boys. Just use her hand or . . .?
C	She just uses her hand.
D	Where does she hit 'em?
C	Cross the back of their legs.
D	Does she? Do any of them ever cry?
C	No. They just sit down and giggle.
D	Do they? *(laughter)*
C	Most of the boys. *(laughter)*
D	And do the girls giggle too?
C	Yes. *(laughter)*
D	Do you talk much when you're not s'posed to? I mean when the teacher can't see you?
C	No. We don't talk much but A . . . E . . ., she's a talker too, and when you talk too much you have to go and sit on a seat all by yourself. And she knows all the noisy group and then they get this big desk, there's room for four, there's usually about four speakers and they put them all together and see how they annoy each other.
D	Oh, I see.
C	That's what she said she was going to do. That's just about all.
D	What do you think is the best time in primary school?
C	Art.
D	Well you thought dictation was probably your best lesson but you like art?
C	Dictation and art.
D	What do you do in art?

C	We um, we've done a dinosaur and we've . . .
D	You all do the same thing do you?
C	Yes, all you do for a dinosaur is you go — do a line across the top and then you do a little line underneath and you join it up, there and there; you do a little line there and you do some feet and . . .
D	So art's really learning how to do things? Who tells you how to do it?
C	Mrs. X.
D	I see. And who are your best friends in the class?
C	C . . . F . . . . G . . . . G . . . . and A . . . E . . . . (*all girls*)
D	I see. And is there anything you really hate about school?
C	(*Long pause*) Mm.
D	Or anything you don't like much?
C	(*Long pause*). Assembly. 'Cause all you do is just stand up and then you say er, "I am an Australian, I love my country, I must obey her laws." Then you just walk into school. I don't like it much.
D	Do you ever see the headmaster?
C	Yes, sometimes.
D	What do you do when he comes in?
C	We be quiet.
D	Do you? (*chuckle*) Why?
C	(*Chuckle*) He's a bit fussy about noise.
D	Is he? Is he a nice man?
C	Yes.
D	Does he know you?
C	Um, I don't know.
D	Do you think he'd know your name is Catherine if he saw you? (*Pause*) You're not frightened of him are you?
C	No.
D	Who's the most frightened . . . Which teacher in the school is the one they're most frightened of?
C	Um, I think about Mrs. Y.
D	Why? Why are they frightened of her?
C	She's a loud mouth.

GOOD GRADE THREE SENTENCES AND A JOINING WORD   37

D   Is she? (*laughter*) What does that mean?

C   (*Laughter*) She's all grumpy and she gives boys really hard smacks.

D   Oh gor!

C   (*Laughter*) She's a loud mouth too. She screams in your ear.

D   And where do you come across her?

C   Oh (*laughter*) She, she's in the classroom next to ours. We can put our ear against the door — Waah! (*laughter*) Yeh. She says (*mimic*) "Excuse me Mrs. X may I talk to your children for a minute?" (*laughter*)

D   Where do you think you come in the class, when they give you reports and things? Are they going to give you a report?

C   Yes at the middle of the year we have all these tests and exams.

D   I see.

C   And all our marks we get we all add them up . . . and that's about all.

D   Where do you think you'll come? Are you worried about it?

C   Oh. Yes, a bit.

D   Why? I mean, you know we don't care. Why would you be worried?

C   I might get a ratbag report.

D   Why? You don't really think so do you?

C   Um. I don't know.

D   What do you think might be bad that Mrs. X might say about you?

C   I don't know.

D   What would be something bad that she could say do you think?

C   Oh, about D . . . K . . . she'd say "Oh, naughty girl, you only got about, you only got sixty . . . you only got . . . you only got eighty for your report."

D   What are some of the good things she'll say about you?

C   Um. I got quite a high report . . . or something, maybe.

D   What about your behaviour? What do you think she'll say about that?

C   Oh, I don't know.

D   Do you think she'll say you work hard?

C	Yes.
D	Do you get homework? Do you ever get homework to do?
C	Yes, but um it's not on papers or anything. Just have to find out about some things. What sort of cross the St. John Ambulance has. What's the number on your er fire hydrant?
D	What do you have to find out those things for?
C	I don't know. Just because it's in our Active English book.
D	What other books do you have to learn out of?
C	Er. Community Helpers Book and we have these Blue Books, that's another one about community helpers. That's all I think.
D	What about maths?
C	Yes, we have maths.
D	Is that easy?
C	Yes. It's quite easy.
D	Do you get ten out of ten for that?
C	Yes, most of the time, I do. You get the very good stamp if you get them all right. Also if you get them all right you have an early minute.
D	Um. What about social studies?
C	Yes, we have social studies. We have to be quiet in that too.
D	What do you do then? You have to be quiet, when?
C	Doing social studies.
D	Well who does the work? Does the teacher talk to you or something?
C	No, we do it all ourselves.
D	What, do you read it out of books or something?
C	Mm.
D	What do you do? What sort of things?
C	Mrs. X helps us a bit. She puts some things on the board and we have to copy it into our book.
D	What sort of things? About what?
C	Um. Communities and things.
D	Is it interesting?
C	Not much.
D	Was it better in infant school? What did you do in infant school?

C	Well, we had um busy books and maths books and um lots of other books.
D	What was good about the infant school? In the learning things you did? Have you forgotten what it was like?
C	Yes.
D	Was it a better teacher?
C	Yes.
D	Why?
C	Um.
D	Why did you like Mrs. M? (*last year's teacher*)
C	Because she was nice and she had a nice laugh and she was kind.
D	Um. Well isn't Mrs. X kind?
C	Yes.
D	Well, she's the same as Mrs. M. then?
C	Um, Mrs. M. was a bit nicer than Mrs. X.

6 *You've just got to be able to tell*

Correct English

Most teachers work on the premise that there is an identifiable entity called "Correct English". The most important thing about it is that everyone knows when you have not got it. But whether you have or have not got it, it has certain properties attributed to it which are in urgent need of questioning.

Correct English is:

- the only way to speak
- the right way to speak
- the best way to speak
- the only way of expressing yourself clearly
- the only language for education
- the only way to achieve precision
- the only language which allows abstraction and conceptualization
- the only logical form of language

If correct English does possess all these properties, then you are in rather an unfortunate position if you don't possess it. You will have no way of speaking, you will be wrong, inferior, unable to express yourself clearly, unable to be educated, unable to be precise, unable to conceptualize and think in abstractions, and you will be illogical. Obviously, you will not do very well at school where it is necessary to be right, to express yourself clearly, be precise, to conceptualize and be logical.

Because many children do not have correct English at their fingertips, and they tend not to do very well at school, it would seem that there are no questions to be asked. It's quite obvious that correct English is essential.

But being a cautious person, I would like to look more closely at this linguistic form, to see exactly what it is which makes it superior, before I give it to those children who don't have it, in order that they, too, might be right, best and . . . logical.

Where Did it Originate?

Where does this correct English come from? Has it always been there or has someone made it up?

Correct English was born with some of the seventeenth century writers such as Dryden. One can only assume that prior to his efforts to draw attention to the correct use of language, people did not know the right way to speak; they were all wrong, inferior and illogical.

Dryden started to correct his own prose, in the twilight years of his life, with the intention of having it resemble more closely the elegance of Latin, which he and his colleagues were trying to emulate.

> "When neo-classical writers like Dryden and Swift started to 'correct' their prose, they were apparently trying to bring English closer to the beauty, clarity and vigor of classical Latin. They looked at their native language as a wild growth that had to be carefully pruned to serve for literary purposes. One way to prune was to condemn features that were at odds with Latin. Latin word order did not allow a preposition at the end of a sentence."[1]

So for generations of school children the rule was born—don't end a sentence with a preposition, because it's not done in Latin, and Dryden didn't like it. One can be forgiven surely, for asking if this is right, best and logical?

Rules of Correctness

There is no great inconsistency between the origins of the first rule of correct English and the ones which were added later. By a process of arbitrary determination different individuals added their own pearls of wisdom and decreed when an error was not an error (a very difficult task given that there was no basis for the decision). So dedicated men laboured on, outlawing illiterate and vulgar uses of the language, and more and more rules were evolved for correct English to ensure that it was right, best and logical.

This is how it was done!

> "When the rules of correctness were codified by the authors of the nineteenth century textbooks, the arguments offered in support were typically *ad hoc* arguments. Apparently logical arguments were

improvised to discredit specific debatable usage, but the same argument was seldom applied across the board to other items of the same kind. Thus respect for etymological derivation was said to require that *between* not be applied to more than two of a kind—since the word was related to both *two* and *twain*."[2]

As I am one who is not sure of all these rules, it still seems dubious to me that this should be the right, the best and the logical way of establishing them!

Personal Prejudices

Because the game was all about "personal preference", then emotional prejudice about language and words began subtly to creep into the rules. Of course, you had to be in a relatively powerful position to start with, if you wanted your prejudices to count. You probably needed to write a book about correct English if you wanted everyone to know that your rules were right, best and logical.

> "A. M. Tibbets has reminded us that L. P. Meredith, the author of *Everyday Errors of Speech* held the degrees of M.D. and D.D.S. and was also author of a possibly more helpful and authoritative treatise on *The Teeth and How to Save Them*."[3]

It is not as if all the rules have been finalized, either. There is still room for people in positions of power and authority to insist that their own peculiar prejudices become sanctified as the right and the best and the logical way of using the English language.

Of course, some people have said that the whole process is unfair. They have dared to challenge the practice of granting so much authority to the dogmatic idiosyncrasies of certain individuals. But, as one would expect under the circumstances, they have been met with the right, best and logical opposition.

> "English professors led the attacks on (these impertinent upstarts who queried the authenticity of correct English) . . . as an 'outrage' or a 'very great calamity'. In a commencement address one orated that such failures to maintain standards of good English were against the whole heritage, even against humanity."[4]

With such reasoned argument against any thoughtful analysis of correct English, the cause is doomed. How can a successful stand be made against the established tradition of correct English when it is confronted by such overwhelming evidence that it is necessary to preserve it for the sake of humanity? Necessary, because in our day to day contact with people *you've got to be able to tell*. You've got to be able to know where they fit in the social hierarchy; you've got to be able to tell their niche. How can we know whether or not to take people seriously unless we have the criteria which lets us know whether they are haves or have nots? It would be disastrous if you met people and you had no way of telling whether they knew the right, the best and the logical. How would you know how to act towards them?

Wearing the Badge

If they are correct in their use of language, then they are wearing a badge, and everyone is comfortable because they can tell who you are. You would have to listen carefully to what people said rather than the way they said it, if you didn't have correct English. It would all just be too confusing!

Correct English then, is not a code which has its origins in linguistics; it has no linguistic validity. It can make no linguistic claim to being the only, right, true, proper and logical way to speak. But it's very useful if you want to make judgments about the relative importance of people; it's a useful tool if you want to know who will do well in school and thereby obtain a privileged position in the social hierarchy; it's very useful as a screening device if you want exclusive membership to the club on the basis of those who know the right, the best and the logical, as you do.

I'd like to conclude with a gentle reminder from the noted linguist, Eric Hamp:

> The whole issue
> ". . . hinges on the word 'correct' or 'proper'; and it is on this point that an enormous and disproportionate amount of confusion has arisen and been perpetuated. . . . Forms such as *aint* and *he don't* are the prevailing forms in any American dialect. From the purely linguistic point of view they are the correct forms in these dialects in the sense that that is what most people normally say. However, in the sense that these forms are not admired and acceptable in certain groups, *they are not 'correct' for the purpose of finding favour with such groups*. But this is a very different form of 'correctness' and the two must not be confused. (My emphasis)."[5]

Notes

1. Guth, Hans P. *English for a New Generation.* McGraw-Hill, 1973, pp. 97-98.
2. Ibid, pp. 98-99.
3. Marckwardt, Albert H. "Language Standards and Attitudes", in Marckwardt, A. H. (ed), *Language and Language Learning.* National Council of Teachers of English, 1968, p. 3.
4. Muller, Herbert, J. *The Uses of English.* Holt, Rinehart and Winston, 1967, p. 59.
5. Hamp, E. P. "Language in a few words; with notes on a re-reading". 1966, in DeCecco,

7 Who has the language deficiency?

Success and Failure

That some students do not succeed at school is an accepted fact in education circles and it is a problem which has attracted many imaginative minds. A number of interesting—even fascinating—explanations have been suggested in an attempt to formulate a solution. The theories have come and gone, but the students who fail education still remain! If we were to believe any of the prophets of gloom among educators and some laymen, who are making dire predictions about the increase of illiteracy, then we would accept that the number of education failures is growing every year.

To try and work out why these students do not do well at school, it seems be quite a logical step to find any common characteristics. It could be a reasonable starting point in trying to establish the causes of success or failure if you could determine what was held in common by all those who fail; and vice versa, what (if any) is the common denominator of those who succeed.

With the intention of "isolating the variables", educators started to look closely at the characteristics of those students who failed education. They began to list the similarities. The next step was to list the differences between those who passed and those who failed.

So the students were put under the microscope; their I.Q.'s were examined, their motivation examined, their family backgrounds examined, their language examined. And the educators were not disappointed. They found what they were looking for. They found that the failures were very similar, and that the failures were very different from the passers.

Those who passed, not only did well in school, they had lots of other favourable achievements as well. They had "better" homes, "better" values, "better" motivation, and "better" language. If you were going to school, it was obviously much "better" to be a member of the group who passed. There were just so many advantages.

And the failures? Well, they found what you might expect. These students failed lots of other things, besides education. They failed to have the things which the passers had. They failed the test on homes and parents; they failed the test on values and motivation. They definitely failed language. There was really no alternative but to find these students all round failures. There were so many things which they lacked. They really were deficient. It was reasonable to describe them as deprived, both culturally and linguistically. Their homes and their language were just not good enough.

Causes of Failure

From classifying these students in this way, it took only one more step to see that the things which they failed outside education were the *cause* of education failure. With sudden insight, the explanation was offered. Because they had deficient/deprived/disadvantaged homes which produced deficient/deprived/disadvantaged language, these students failed education. It was quite a logical rationale for education failure.

The explanation for education failure found ready acceptance. Those who passed came from good homes, and had good language in their possession. Those who failed came from deficient homes and were the victims of language deficiency. Language is the medium of education. If your language was deficient, then you failed education. Logical and plausible. There were few vociferous dissenters.

Having found the cause of education failure, the policy makers in education were morally bound to do something to rectify the situation. It would have been an awkward move to attempt to change the deficient homes that the failures came from. But there was nothing to prevent educators from changing the deficient language. With self-righteous determination policies were formulated to change the deficient language of the students who failed.

"Overcoming" Language Deficiency

With unwavering conviction, educators began devising programs, called "compensatory education programs", aimed at changing the deficient language of the failures into the same proficient language of the passers. Once the failures had the same language as the passers, there would be no problem. Education failure would rightly become a thing of the past. Those students who failed could be given the language of those who passed, and thereby become passers themselves!

So there was confrontation with the language of the failures. With justification, teachers began an assault on the language of the failures. They began to take away the language which these students had, and to attempt to put another language in its place. That the students might not want this new language was never seriously considered. The educators were convinced that they would have it.

Through educational institutions, failure students were subjected to this treatment. Like medicine which was good for them, they were dosed with this new and better language. The diagnosticians stood back and waited for the treatment to take effect. They waited for the end of education failure.

Quite obviously they are still waiting. There are those educators who are claiming that the patient, rather than improving, is actually deteriorating. The prescription did not work; unfortunately the patient was not cured. What had gone wrong?

This is when awkward questions began to be asked. In the whole expensive exercise of compensatory education to get rid of all the language deficiency, no one had stopped to ask the fundamental question — what does language do, how does it work? Had these questions been asked, and adequately answered, then the term "language deficiency" may never have been coined. Because there is no doubt that it is an inaccurate term!

What have we done to those students who were subjected to the callous act of being deprived of their own language for learning, and having forcibly replaced with something which was artificial, on an erroneous premise? What is the need for "compensation" now?

> "That educational psychology should be strongly influenced by a theory so false to the facts of language is unfortunate; but that children should be the victims of this ignorance is intolerable. It may seem that the fallacies of the verbal deprivation theory are so obvious that they are hardly worth exposing . . . (but). . . it is an important job for us to undertake."[1]

There are just too many imaginative leaps in the systematized verbal deprivation theory. Fallacy number one is that there is one way of using language which is better than any other — the way that the education passers do. Which comes first, the chicken or the egg? The linguists have accumulated a substantial body of evidence to support the linguistic premise that the language of every individual is good for him — it meets his needs. The language of each individual allows him to manipulate his environment.

Common Sense

Could we possibly be practical? Could we just have a simple look at language? Do you really believe that because you say "aint" and "we was" you are less able to understand the education of the school? Do you really think that "yous" cannot make meanings?

Every normal person learns to talk. Every school child comes to school with his language. It is a language which he has developed within his own context to meet his needs, to mediate his environment. All normal school children are capable of making themselves understood in their own language. In this sense, they are linguistically competent.

Language competence is the knowledge of language which allows every individual to make up an infinite number of sentences, to create language. There is no limit to the number of sentences an individual can create. All normal native speakers of a language possess this ability—they differ in the forms which they choose to implement it. They differ in the ways in which they put language competence into practice.

Language performance is the execution of this competence and each individual has his own translation. Performance is not governed by competence only; it can be determined by habit, emotion, context, mood, personality traits. These are not linguistic features.

As educators, it seems that language competence is something with which we should be concerned. But perhaps we have not seen beyond language performance—idiosyncratic language habits. Perhaps we have spent too much time on the form and not enough on the substance.

Is there any difference between the language of education passers and education failures, that is more than just habit? Is it just that the passers have the nicer habits? Is it just that their table manners are more pleasing—when they are like your own?

Do the education passers achieve their school success because they have a language necessary for education; or is the language the passing factor?

If education were dominated by individuals who had little respect for the written word, the education failures would be those who did. If it were dominated by those who valued emotion beyond intellect, then the deficient students would be those who could not reach emotional peaks. If it were dominated by those who thought life more important than learning, then perhaps the serious scholar would fail education.

But this is mere speculation. Education is not dominated by any of these things. It is dominated by a group which values the language it has learned, and yes, those who do not possess it are the education failures—they just do not have the same language habits. They have *no deficiencies*; they are simply not the same.

Who Has the Language Deficiency?

To coerce those who have different linguistic habits from the teachers to acquire those of the teacher—to enforce conformity—may be educationally justifiable if you cannot tolerate those who have different habits. It would be justifiable if teachers are quite sure that they have a monopoly on gracious living and that there are measurable advantages in practising their particular life style; that is that they are happier, more fulfilled, better adjusted, more mature individuals precisely because they possess such

48 THE SPITTING IMAGE

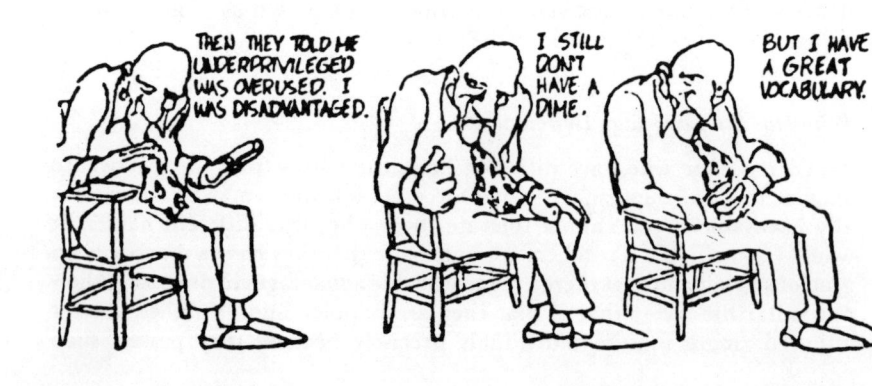

habits. If teachers can demonstrate that their linguistic habits bring peace of mind, then I am all for teaching these to the kids.

This, however, is not the basis of the language deficiency theory. This is not the basis of depriving a child of his own language, the language by which he learns. It is not the rationale for education failure.

Who has the language deficiency? Those who are so rigid that they cannot tolerate habits which are not their own?

Who needs compensatory education? Those whose views are sufficiently limited to label difference as deficiency and failure?

Who has the answer?

> "Teachers must simply abandon the theory that usages differ in quality, as between good and bad, correct and incorrect, and instead build their methods and reconstruct their emotional reactions on the plain facts that are already known in part to their pupils . . . the learner has an indefensible right to speak as he likes without school penalties, while the teacher has no rights in this respect but only the duty to demonstrate what usages are profitable in the adult world."[2]

Notes

1. Labov, W. "The Logic of Non-Standard English", in *Language in Education*. Open University Source Book, London, Routledge & Paul, 1972, p. 210.

2. Joòs, Martin. "Language and the School Child", in *Harvard Educational Review*, 34 (2), 1964, p. 209.

8 There is no such thing as linguistic sin

Learning the Rules

My parents speak very well. When I was a child I was sent to elocution classes so that I too would speak well. It was never that my grammar was wrong, *that* was tediously mastered in the early years; it was that my vowel sounds were too broad. I had an Australian accent. It grated on the sensitive ears of those around me.

Life began each morning with speech exercises, designed to keep me on the straight and narrow linguistic path. Behaviour problems in my environment were defined by my mother's pained facial expression when I requested a "cupper tea" or volunteered that I was "gonna plaiy with a fren".

I tell you all this so that you will know how well I was taught, and how nicely I spoke. There could be no doubts about my articulation, my grammar or my vocabulary.

When I was an adolescent, I could listen with slight distaste to those around me who found it necessary to resort to such vulgarities as "King" and "Gas" and "Fab" to describe their weekend entertainments. My Saturdays were always "rewarding" and my Sundays "rejuvenating".

When I became an adult, I recognized that I used the language of those around me as a form of social barometer. When they spoke I operated my own screening device to distinguish the acceptable from the unacceptable. I was the product of a well-spoken home environment. My language prejudices were reinforced by my contact with a university English department. There was no doubt that I was well versed in the linguistic catechism. I believed in linguistic sin.

Then I became a teacher, an English teacher.

The Classroom Assault

I took my sophisticated linguistic repertoire to the classroom and proceeded to commence my indoctrination courses. I took my screening device and found that the pressure was too great for it. It became overloaded in trying to separate the acceptable from the unacceptable.

My primary interest in the classroom was to survive. My pedantic notions of language usage made life in the classroom almost intolerable. I physically shuddered almost every time a student addressed me. I was constantly offended by the way in which they spoke. Obviously there was a limit to my capacity to endure the assault on my linguistic sensitivity; something had to change.

Either I sacrificed myself in the interest of linguistic purity and standards, or I sacrificed some of the standards, in order to make classroom life more bearable.

I opted for the latter. I made a deliberate effort to ignore some of the linguistic sins of my students. I made a conscious effort to concentrate on the matter instead of the form.

This did help my tolerance span considerably. Sometimes I could even manage a whole lesson without my hackles rising. I ignored the petty misdemeanours and concentrated on the "gross" sins which I felt I had a responsibility to eradicate.

So my first few years of teaching found me reducing the number of linguistic sins. I retained the ones which were grave, but I desensitized myself to the extent that I could accept that there were some unacceptable language uses which were relatively trivial. I decided I could afford not to notice. I was quite pleased with my tolerant and broad minded approach. I was comfortable in my ability to be flexible.

But my elocution teacher and the university English department were a long way away by this time. Although they had had me for my formative years, I had passed from their jurisdiction. They no longer exerted direct influence over me. I began to have doubts.

Old Questions — New Answers

Questions began to arise in the classroom, the staffroom and some of the "new" literature I now found. And I began to find these questions increasingly difficult to put behind me. I began to question my linguistic faith.

Why was it that I could emerge laughing, from teaching the "lowest" class in the school, where for forty minutes I had been regaled with the weekend's hilarious fiasco of a fishing trip? Why was I captivated by these students explaining to me about the dangers of diving in the creek for golf balls? Why could I enjoy their tales and their yarns?

And why did I have difficulty trying to stay awake in the "better" classes, during an oral lesson? Why did I find their stories without colour? Why did I find their talks so dry and uninspiring?

Once you forget the form and listen for the essence, what is it that you find? When you allow students the penalty free environment to use their own language, why is it that the non-academic stream in the school shows a greater power over language than many of those who are winning the school achievement prizes?

It was difficult to reconcile my list of linguistic sins with the linguistic sinners. There were too many pieces that just would not fit.

I began to make tapes and to listen carefully to the language of my students. If it was a love of words, an ease with language, a vitality and enthusiasm that I sought then I needed an oral lesson with a "below average ability" group. If however, I wished to be embarrassed for the speaker, if I wished to experience self-consciousness with language, I could embark on an oral lesson with the academic stream, listening to the tedious, ritualistic lecturettes and being plagued to give marks.

Revelation

The language of the below average kids was frequently refreshing, while the tension which accompanied oral language in some of the more privileged groups was frequently exhausting.

It was a revelation to find myself in the position where I saw the "better" speakers in need of my assistance. I found myself a convert to the doctrine that language works, it makes meanings, when you can forget about all the rules.

If I had any missionary zeal left, I think I would see the linguistic, rule ridden forms of the academic classes as a challenge. I think I would like to save them from their linguistic convolutions and contortions and help them to free themselves from the artificial codes in which they find themselves so often enmeshed. But it's almost too soon for me yet. I'm just beginning my own escape.

Of course I have not forgotten those linguistic sins in which I was indoctrinated as a child and a student. They have not disappeared. I still flinch when confronted with horrendous grammatical errors and "careless" speech. But I'm beginning to be able to laugh at myself now. I'm trying to cast off those debilitating rules and regulations and to get back to the language which is close to me. I'm trying to get rid of the pretence and I find that language works more easily every day.

If kids are going to master language, then teachers must abandon the concept of linguistic sin. It tangles them up too much, it ties them in so many knots. It confuses by placing the emphasis on *how*, instead of *what* is said. Give them the opportunity to find that their language works.

Why can't they be like me? 9

Name:	Dale Spender
Age:	Somewhere in the thirties (early).
Address:	Good middle class area.
Father's Occupation:	Accountant.
Own Occupation:	University lecturer.
Hobbies:	Reading, writing, talking.
Comment:	Successful product of the education system. Good table manners. Speaks nicely.

My occupation has not always been university lecturer. Until fairly recently it was listed as English teacher, and as an English teacher I had all the predictable characteristics. Because I was trained in a university English department I was familiar with all the good books, able to make value judgments about writing, knew style when I saw it, and was dedicated to bringing poetry into the lives of all those whom I encountered. An average English teacher you might say.

I began my career as an English teacher with an inbuilt hierarchy which placed Jane Austen and George Eliot at the top and ranged down through Dickens, Hardy and Joyce to "commercial trash" which included everything from Raymond Chandler to Agatha Christie and comics. I did not feel an outsider in the English staffroom when I first started teaching.

To me, reading and writing are enjoyable acts. I plan my time to allow me to indulge in the pleasures of reading and writing. A world without books is the worst thing I can think of. I find my hobby is reading, my relaxation is reading, and my job means reading. You can guess by now, I rate it fairly highly on my list of priorities. And I was no different when I first started teaching in a comprehensive secondary school.

My entrance to teaching was marked by goodwill, idealism and a sense of responsibility. There was no doubt in my mind that I was going to share the fruits of my labour with the students whom I was destined to teach. Translated, that means that I was determined that these students would learn to understand and to share my love of the written word.

'That book we found you reading has corrupted me, Smith.'

With banner held high, I entered every classroom with the intention of giving the students the wonderful experiences (which I had had) of reading and writing. I was committed to my cause and my faith did not waver.

I was a diligent teacher. I spent many hours preparing my teaching aids; I made charts, collected pictures, made tapes, rewrote endings, drew characters, structured "situations". I did everything I possibly could to make "literature live" and to fire my students with enthusiasm, so that they would take up the challenge and go out and read!

The hardest lesson I had to learn was that so many of them did not want to! It is a lesson I haven't learnt very well.

I felt I had something of value for my students; I knew that many other people also thought it was of value; I knew I was being paid to help my students see that value and I made a strenuous effort to communicate that value. Right was on my side, and yet some of the students did not want it. What I offered the students was rejected by many, and I did not readily adjust to this. I was both disturbed and distressed by my reception. I was frustrated when they did not want to hear my message.

I looked at some of the students who could not read, who felt "failures", who were labelled with the stigma of "remedial reading", who constantly said "we can't do that miss, we're dumb." And I thought *I* had an answer.

I listened to students who recounted their weekend activities to me; they told me of meetings around the juke box in the milk bar, of hours spent in front of the television, of days when they "had nothing to do" and I thought how all would be transformed if they could read. I diagnosed a need for "constructive leisure habits" and I prescribed books. And I tried desperately to convince them.

But they either wouldn't or couldn't read. And I couldn't just blame myself. The remedial reading teacher couldn't teach them, despite all her training, hardware and software. And they wouldn't be taught by other English teachers either! Often I would think that they were dumb, if they couldn't see the sense of my arguments, but I thought such a judgment was unfair.

It was almost as if their resistance was directly related to my efforts. The more I filled the classroom with the need to read, the more "behaviour problems" I had. There was constant escalation as I increased my efforts to bring them reading, and they increased their rejection. I even entertained the vague notion that despite my dedication, my good intentions and my good works, some of them were moving further away from reading. My common sense, however, would not allow me to dwell on such a preposterous idea.

I often felt cheated and resentful. There were so few rewards in my first years of teaching and yet I had wanted to do so much and I had genuinely tried so hard. Obviously there were other teachers who shared my experience.

> "Many . . . teachers, having experienced success themselves, have a genuine wish to make all children share in it too. They are often committed to liberal and progressive educational ideals. Yet they find it hard to believe that everyone is not motivated by the same carrots which were held out to them. When they encounter children whose goals and values are different from theirs, and whose pace and method of working are unfamiliar, they are often shocked and may feel themselves rejected. They find it hard to believe that their careful plans of work, based on approaches which have succeeded for them, and arising out of a genuine concern for the children's learning, can be unacceptable."[1]

I kept asking myself what's wrong with these kids, why can't they understand how necessary and important reading is, why won't they learn? Are they perverse and self destructive? Why can't they be like me?

Whenever there was the fleeting suggestion that they couldn't understand how I could waste my spare time reading and I couldn't understand how they could waste theirs watching television or congregating in the local milk bar, I was able to conveniently dismiss it without undue effort or rationalization.

After all, I knew I was right! Everywhere in educational circles my value system was reinforced. Whenever I emerged bruised from the classroom I would always be revived by some sympathetic colleague who was equally convinced of the value and validity of reading, someone who was equally determined that the students *would* learn to see it that way too. The Education Department considered it important enough to provide the school with a remedial reading teacher and a smorgasbord of remedial teaching aids. All the teachers knew the kids had to learn to read.

Society knew it too. The Sunday papers popularized the literacy scare with its sensational "kids don't read as well as they used to" and this was fuel enough to send me back to the classroom again. I made more aids and performed more antics. But it was like seed sown on barren ground. With true self-righteousness I often looked at my ungrateful students and thought that they did not deserve my energy and talents.

What were they? Lazy, stupid, apathetic or pure bloody minded?

There had to be a day of reckoning. One day, after a failed "guaranteed to turn you on" sequence I returned to the staffroom with the grim knowledge that if I didn't soon find a solution, there would be a limited number of places that my friends would find me. There were some vague unarticulated questions lurking beneath my convictions, and I had to face them. The doubts could no longer be repressed.

If I were to take a genuine look at reading, and the kids, it meant first looking at me and my teaching. And I found that prospect frightening! I had to start with what I was, and what I was doing if I were to adequately dispel the doubts. I had postponed the soul searching for too long.

Bit by harrowing bit I looked in the mirror and saw the middle-class teacher who flaunted into the classroom each day in her good middle class clothes, with her good middle class accent, her good middle class manners, her good middle class values and her good middle class *panacea*. And some children did not see the world in the way that she saw it.

To those children who did not share her view of the world, she loudly shouted in her every movement and word *you will learn to be more like me*! Of course, she was more subtle than to write it on the board. She hid the message behind a masquerade of gimmicks, tricks, carrots and whips called teaching strategies. But she didn't ever change the message. It was the same lesson every day.

She went into the classroom and told those students, from Monday to Friday, that they were missing out on something. She told them that they were not like her. With monotonous regularity she told them that they wouldn't amount to anything *unless they became as she was.* And no-one ever told her she was arrogant. Those kids were very polite.

"A further limiting characteristic of the traditional education of most . . . teachers is that elitist view of culture which is common in schools and society alike. It may be that the (teacher's) struggle to achieve examination success has been at the cost of a more spontaneous and dynamic response to experience . . . all will have been sacrificed to the need to meet the external demand of formal 'learning'. The (teacher) in this situation may have found it difficult to establish and keep alive a personal and genuine concern for a broadly based view of culture. . . . The young teacher's genuine disappointment at the children's rejection of the cultural values he has to offer—which he may interpret as evidence of laziness, apathy or bloody mindedness—may merely reflect the narrowness of his own view of what culture can be."[2]

It is not an easy lesson to learn that not everyone sees the same world as I do. It's not easy to stop telling them to be more like me if they want to live in my world. I wonder if there will ever be a meeting ground where I will appreciate their milk bars, and they will appreciate my books?

Like the missionary, I remain firm in my belief of the superiority of my god, and I suppose I still want to convert the heathen so that they may find Paradise. But coercion and carrots are subterfuge. They must find their own faith. Though it's hard to leave them alone. I have to stop thinking that I have a right to interfere. I'm not a missionary, I'm a teacher, someone who doesn't possess all the secrets. I know it's not absolutely necessary that *they all be like me*!

Notes

1. Hannan, Charles, Smyth, Pat, and Stephenson, Norman. *Young Teachers and Reluctant Learners.* Penguin Papers in Education, 1972, pp. 20-21.
2. Ibid, pp. 22-23.

10 How many languages do you need?

Who is to Blame?

It is always the English teacher who is to blame! When the history teacher finds that the class cannot write essays . . . "What do they teach you in English these days?". When the science teacher notices that the kids cannot spell . . . "What do you do in English?". The tradition in the school is that if it is anything to do with reading and writing, then it is the English teacher who is the expert.

This, like many other assumptions which have been made about language, is largely erroneous. Reading and writing are not service skills. There is no great universal literacy machine into which the English teacher can feed the rules, and out of which comes reading and writing, which can be readily utilized in any subject area. To think that reading and writing can be taught in vacuo, is to think that students can read reading, and write writing. At school, you can write history, read geography, write science experiments, read economics texts. And for better or worse at the moment, each subject has its own linguistic code.

Horses for Courses

If you want kids to be able to use the language of science (and that is another assumption that I would like to question later), or read civics, then it is the science teacher and the civics teacher who must teach them to do so. English teachers, though their specialty may be words, do not see the world the way the scientist does, nor in fact, the way the civics' teacher does. Their use of language has evolved from their own interests, their own training, and their own knowledge; in this case, probably extensive study in English literature.

The science teacher, on the other hand, functions within the framework of the language of science which has evolved as the subject has become "institutionalized". Science has developed its own way of looking at the world which involves a form of linguistic shorthand and jargon, peculiar to scientists.

For example, imagine four people, an engineer, a geologist, an artist and an historian who have all been shown a great big rock. The ways in which they see that rock will depend greatly on the subject area which they feel committed to. I am stretching my own imagination in trying to speculate on the ways in which each of them would use the language of their own subject to describe the rock.

To the engineer, it may present an interesting problem; it may be that he sees it as future foundations or as something to be moved, perhaps even as something which may be utilized. The geologist could perhaps be more interested in the composition of the rock itself, in its distinguishing marks and lines, its origins and the processes to which it has been subjected. The form, texture, colour and line would be the predominating concerns of the artist, who may simply let the rock suggest something else. To the historian, there may also be an imaginative act involved, but it will differ substantially from the imagination of the artist. The historian may wish to know the secrets of the rock; he may wish to know the events that it has witnessed; he may wonder how it has been used by man. Which rock is it?

Of course, with mature adults who have command over their language, it is perhaps possible to make the leap from the language of one subject area to another (some teachers teach more than one subject). But this demands expertise in the language and calls for many imaginative acts at times.

If anyone could legislate on which individual is seeing the right rock, or if there were a superior individual who could master the language sufficiently so that he could encompass the four languages which viewed the rock, then it is quite possible that English teachers could teach students to write biology essays. In default of a legislator or a superior being, it seems unlikely that these feats can be accomplished and it may be the biology teacher who has to teach kids to write biology essays.

That is, if you think biology essays should be written in the language of the biologist.

The Science Lesson

I was once watching a group of students in a science laboratory. They were classified as low level ability students and their teacher had tried to introduce some science experiments which he thought they would enjoy. His efforts were being rewarded and the kids were quite involved and enthusiastic about what they were doing.

They had to put a bunsen burner under a beaker and evidently something strange and interesting would happen. The group of kids whom

I was observing were denied that experience. The boy who was holding the bunsen burner leant across the bench, balancing precariously on his stool, in the attempt to place it under the beaker. He did not manage to retain his balance, and as he slipped to the floor, almost in slow motion, he managed to take with him the practical books of two students, an assortment of writing implements, one other student and the precious beaker. The bunsen burner did extinguish itself during its descent so there was little damage.

Having sorted out the mess and soothed the ruffled tempers, the teacher went on to perform the experiment for the kids and the yellow substance in the beaker changed to blue. If they did not find that an anticlimax, they certainly found the way they were required to write up the experiment both anticlimactic and mystifying.

In the impersonal language of the scientist these kids struggled to use the passive voice to describe what had happened. The "activity" was too close to them. They became confused and showed evidence of strain as they tried to forget their involvement in the fiasco and concentrate on being "detached". And I could not help but wonder if it was necessary.

Would the science book have been defiled in any way if the experiment were to be written up as follows:

> "We were doing an experiment in science. Bill had the bunsen burner to go under the beaker so we could find out what happened, but he fell off his chair before he could get there. He knocked Sally onto the floor and everybody's books landed up all over the place. I couldn't find my pencil and had to search all over the floor for it for ages. Mr Jones got pretty upset at first and then he knew it was an accident and he helped us to fix it up again. This time it worked and the stuff in the beaker changed colour. He said it always did this when it got hot. It was a very bright blue."

I don't think that the kids would have had nearly as much difficulty in writing in this way. Of course, it is not the language of science, but I would want to ask

- is the experiment more meaningful when written up in the language of science, and
- did the students need the language of science?

I am not disputing that scientists have their own language and that it is necessary. It is for this reason that I would assert that only science teachers can teach it. What I am querying is the use of such language in school, where the kids are not scientists, but simply kids.

And remember, they probably "do" five or six subjects, each with its own linguistic requirements. I have already stated that it involved an imaginative act on my part to theorize on what the engineer, the geologist, the artist and the historian would see in the rock. Yet each day, kids are asked to be, on the demand of a buzzer, anything from economist through geographer to scientist. How many languages do we think they need? How many times are we going to use language to hinder instead of to facilitate learning?

Try Learning their Language

Believing that the art of effective communication lies in simplicity, I am always disturbed when I find language used to complicate things. Knowing that language is essential for learning, I find it an irrational process to insist that children learn in a language which they do not readily possess.

When sophisticated linguistic forms are prescribed as essential for comprehension and learning, and yet children do not have access to such forms, then I suggest that either

- the teacher ceases to view learning as his objective, or
- the linguistic forms which are prescribed be abandoned.

It would seem that one solution is more acceptable than the other!

This is in no way an argument against teaching kids to use the language of specific subjects. On the contrary it is because the language of each subject is highly differentiated and specialised that I think that all teachers are language teachers within their own subject area. But the complex and differentiated linguistic forms which are an integral part of each subject are characteristics of the mature scientist, geologist or economist. If you are none of these then perhaps you do not need to be able to speak in these precise terms. If you are a kid in school, then perhaps the best language is that of a kid in school. Perhaps the easiest way to learn is to use your own language. That may be the only language that you need!

11 How to stop kids reading

Given the current state of research into reading failure and reading reluctance, we cannot be certain about methods which will work. Still, encouraged by people like Kenneth Goodman, Herbert Kohl and Frank Smith, we suggest that some of the following strategies should ensure continuing reading failure.

Don't let kids cheat

If you find kids who like books so much that they learn them off by heart and then sit around "making out" to read, intervene. They could develop a good feeling towards books but it's a dangerous habit, like swimming with one foot on the bottom. It's better to instil a fear of drowning and to warn them away from the deep end. With luck they will never swim and never drown, because they'll never go near water.

Don't let kids guess

This is nearly as bad as cheating. We know that good readers guess all the time so that they can go fast and understand what they are reading. Therefore, the best way to make sure kids don't understand what they are reading is to ban guessing. In this way the kid's mind will always be on the word which is tagged by the jerking finger. What came before will be forgotten and so it will be impossible to predict what's coming next. Reading will then be a kind of absurdist steeplechase with no flat and no winning post.

Insist that they read out loud

If you have voyeuristic instincts, if you want to monitor the nightmare steeplechase of the mind, then you are advised to make the kids read aloud to you, preferably from a graded reader. It will also help if the graded reader is nonsensical. It should not be hard to find a good selection of such readers.

As the kids read aloud you should be alert to intervene and teach appropriate hurdle attack skills. This might slow them down but it will make them methodical, cautious and on-guard at each hurdle. The important thing is not that they win but that they get over the hurdle even if they have to get off and lift the horse over.

Reading aloud makes guessing almost impossible for young readers. It also makes sure that the reader goes so slow that comprehension is out of the question. When you read in your head, you can go straight from the symbols on the page to meaning, but when you read out loud, you have to sound out each word. This makes it more complicated. Of course, really good readers, like Sir John Gielgud, can guess ahead so fast that they can then put character and expression and music into their words. Don't expect more than a monotone from most young readers.

The beauty of the reading aloud game is that it is quite divorced from anything that happens in the real world, where you only read aloud to others if you have found something interesting, or if you want to give them instructions, or if you want to entertain them. The kids will rightly perceive the game as a test in which they have to read to someone who already knows the story which is not worth knowing anyway.

Get upset about errors

When teaching kids to read, develop a hatred of error. Show joy, even rapture, when right responses are made. Be outwardly sympathetic when the kid is wrong but show that deep down you are hurt.

Take maximum precautions to avoid error. Give the kids trite, repetitive material and never allow them to read above their present level. Teach them in advance how to avoid error. This will ensure that they rarely get the chance to learn by their mistakes and that they will learn to depend on you and look to you for clues. It will also convince them that reading is a difficult game, full of snares and hidden trip-wires.

Be clinical and technological

You must know the anatomy of reading. The best way to render the body disfunctional is to anatomize it. After anatomizing, of course, the body is dead. Therefore in the interest of humanity it is advisable to practise anatomy on already dead bodies. Knowledge gained in this way can then be applied in the diagnosis and prescription of remedies for live bodies.

As a reading teacher you can consider yourself a specialist, like a brain surgeon or a chiropractor, and therefore it is proper to invent special terms to describe special ailments and to draw up a taxonomy of symptoms.

You will need batteries of tests, reading laboratories, tachistoscopes, flash cards and graded materials; reading rate controllers; word builders; visual and aural stimuli and the full spectrum of reading schemes from words in colour to braille for beginners.

Laboratories are particularly useful because they generally bear greater resemblance to diagnostic reading tests than to books. Therefore practice in the reading laboratory usually makes kids good at doing reading tests. In this way, you can give your client the elation of living, even if it is in a kind of iron lung.

As an expert of the new technology, you should be at pains to avoid simple remedies which have worked in the past such as getting kids interested in wanting to read.

'We must bear in mind that the vast majority of pupils are below average ability.'

Find out the kids' reading age

While testing for IQ has fallen into disrepute, you will be pleased to know that testing for reading age is still "in". As a matter of fact, it is undergoing a startling renaissance with the advent of the literacy scare.

Of course, reading age tests are not scientifically valid, but they are useful in all sorts of ways: to provide ammunition for politicians, principals and parents; to support requests for streaming according to ability; to explain educational failure and to underline the need for specialist reading teachers.

Furthermore, despite the invalidity of the tests, it is surprising how quickly kids adjust their reading performance once *you* know what their reading age is supposed to be. In cases where a kid continues to defy the test results by reading stuff he shouldn't be able to read, you may have to disclose the reading age to other teachers and in the last resort to the parents.

You don't have to tell the kids their reading age so long as you group them according to reading age (e.g., red group, green group, purple group, black group). They will then quickly work it out for themselves. If you haven't tried this strategy, you can be sure it will fulfil all your expectations.

Choose their friends for them and test each friendship

Just as some parents try to choose or to censor the friends of their children, as a reading teacher you should at least make sure that comics, magazines, bestsellers and books from home are not allowed into the school. These are undesirable and seductive and kids are likely to read them during lessons.

At secondary level, in particular, *you* should bring the *best* people into the classroom and insist that everyone gets to know them. For instance, make everyone read *The Hobbit* and then ask lots of questions.

Indeed, it should be standard practice to ask comprehension questions at the end of any reading. You can't just trust that they have read it. Detective-type questions are better than general questions where they might be able to get away with a general knowledge of the story.

Some reserve strategies which might work

- Be anxious about their failure to read and convey your anxiety to the kids.
- Keep sending kids who can't read to do more reading. It's good reinforcement to get kids practising what they fail at.
- Give grades for reading. Preferably you should have a Principal or Headmistress to hear the reading.
- Don't allow talking in the library.
- Don't read much yourself.
- Use text books in which the language is dull, impersonal and clinical.
- Never allow kids to read their own stories or messages to others.
- *Above all, on a national scale* . . . provide more and more remedial reading teachers. Then you will have people who continually need poor readers in order to practise.

How to start kids reading

Kids have been learning to read in Australia since the first settlement; in private schools and state schools, in staid schools and "mod" schools, in outback homesteads and circus caravans. Indeed, many have learnt to read despite the fact that they have been taught by people following the advice given above. How kids learn to read is still very much a mystery.

Various methods and materials have come and gone; various schemes have had their day; various research findings have been feted and fated.

But three things at least have remained constant:

- Kids at five or six still expect to learn to read.
- Teachers (and parents) still set out to teach kids to read.
- People still write books and articles and newspaper reports and instructions and menus and signs for other people to read.

Perhaps the present reading panic in Australia has diverted attention from these three constants.

While we hear demands for more teachers trained in the methodology of teaching reading, for more equipment and for more sophisticated monitoring of national standards, the truth might be that we need more patient teachers who can read well, who enjoy reading and who like kids; teachers who know that we read to get meanings which will inform, instruct or entertain us.

Could it be that too much knowledge about the techniques of teaching reading gets in the way of effective teaching? Could it be, as Herbert Kohl suggests, that anyone who can read can teach anyone else to read, given patience and a desire to read on the part of the learner? Could it be that intuition, commonsense and concern are the basic ingredients of a good reading teacher? Could it be that the last thing we need is an expert? Whatever answers you may give, you would no doubt agree that there is no one method that will guarantee success.

Nevertheless, a correspondent to a national women's magazine recently produced a novel suggestion which has at least as much merit as the panaceas that have been peddled in the past. She suggests that since kids seemed to learn to read in the unsophisticated days of outside lavatories (and newspaper squares on a nail), we might consider serialising children's classics on toilet paper. Thus we could provide a subtle enticement to the reluctant reader who is always asking to be excused.

While this is a rather flippant suggestion, it provides some lessons for the teacher. In the first place, reading is an essentially private human activity, often practised in leisure and undertaken in a secure environment. In the second place much reading begins with and is sustained by curiosity and interest. In the third place, reading is most likely to continue if the material has been voluntarily chosen by the reader. Finally, we learn by doing the real thing; we learn to read by reading.

Missing in the above analysis is the teacher. No one would deny that once kids decide they want to read, teachers can help. We know that some kids teach themselves to read before they come to school, but it seems that most children would not achieve literacy without help from another.

It has already been implied that if you aspire to be a good reading teacher, you might practise the antitheses of the "how-not-to" advice above. This is not necessarily so. If the teacher likes the kids; if they like the teacher; if the teacher believes that a certain method will work and if they believe she knows what she is doing, then they will probably learn to read.

Possibly the most profound mistake a reading teacher can make is to teach reading instead of kids. Unfortunately we are today bedevilled by far too many teachers who have failed to be humble before the mysteries of the reading process, while making a mystique of reading technology.

As an antidote, the following notes are offered with a pinch of agnosticism and with hope for a better future.

- The greatest cause of reading failure is failure to read. Therefore, the reading teacher should exude confidence that the kids will learn to read. Plenty of happy early reading experiences are needed.

- A good start may be to do what many mums and dads do; read to them often and well.

- They come to school not with blank minds but with a wealth of living experiences and language abilities. Ideally, their talking should be linked with their reading and their reading should be close to their experiences and their fantasies.

- Kids love hearing stories and telling stories. Stories they tell can be turned into books for them to read.

- Above all, the teaching of reading should show that reading is natural (in a civilised way) and easy. In the real world, reading is everywhere. Before the kids come to school, they have a good deal of experience of the written word and of seeing people reading. Therefore, what they first learn to read should be *real* reading; real meanings made by real writers for real readers. Meaningless material teaches wrong attitudes towards reading and towards school.

Notes

See:

Goodman, Kenneth. "Effective Teachers of Reading Know Language and Children", *Elementary English*. September, 1974, pp. 823-828.

Kohl, Herbert. *Reading, How to*. Bantam Books, New York, 1973.

Smith, Frank. *Understanding Reading; a Psycholinguistic Analysis of Reading and Learning to Read*. Holt, Rinehart and Winston, New York, 1971.

12 Wanking with words

What do English teachers learn about literature from their university lecturers? Are university English departments good examples of how to treat literature? Has anyone made a study of what goes on in teaching and learning in our universities?

These questions are products of my pique. You are warned, therefore, that what follows is more the result of my spleen and my memory than of my detached consideration of the present reality of Australian universities. I did not enjoy English at university and I think I have since learnt to reject almost everything I learnt.

The Cultural Heritage Fallacy

I have learnt to reject the *Cultural Heritage Fallacy* that literature is the sacred transmitter of *Culture*, a view based on a static model of literature and the belief that the reader is passive. It fails to recognize that literature only survives while it is subversive or at least a challenge to the world of today. I believe that we quarry the literature of the past, not to find culture but to find resources which will help us build a new culture. What we preserve in literature, we choose to preserve because it helps us to cope with ourselves and our world.

Those teachers still trapped by the myth of Cultural Heritage are at once self-satisfied and tense. Self-satisfied, because they have *the truth*; tense because they must be ever vigilant to exclude the masquerader and the charlatan. The Pantheon must be kept pure. The proponents of this model are often inclined to the view that today's world is degenerate and should be abandoned.

The Moral Fallacy

I have learnt also to reject the *moral fallacy* which asserts that literature, like castor oil, is good for us; that by drinking deeply of the work of fine minds, we shall become better, more honest, more sensitive and more altruistic beings. Steiner[1] has exploded this myth with his accounts of the reading habits of many Nazi war leaders and, no doubt, you too could point to some professors of English literature who would admit to some peccadilloes, at least.

There is no need to labour the unpleasant effects of the moral fallacy in our schools. You have almost certainly met those insufferable teachers who, like pharmacists, dispense great works to their ailing and indigent students. You know, too, the usual response of the students.

I am not sure that I picked up the *"future value" fallacy* at university but there is no doubt that I used to work on some kind of deferred gratification principle. Deep inside I had to believe that one day I would be able to enjoy books. Anyway, I have now learnt the fallacy of future value. In schools, however, many students are still made to learn Macbeth's soliloquies by heart because teacher knows that one day in the future they will be glad of it.

Poor students.

"Man never is but always to be blest."

Literary Criticism

Are the universities to blame for humble teachers who treat poets and writers as revered and superior beings; for perplexed teachers who agonize over lists of great writers in order like a premiership table; for lost teachers who claim to love literature while leading miserable lives? Do universities take a too precious attitude to literature? Have they failed to see the fuller significance of "storying" both as a social act and as an innate need for all men?

Joe Spriggs argues that there is something rotten in the "Eng Lit" department and his canny nose sniffs out the bona fide "lit critter", addicted to constant shots of writing about writing. "The language of lit crit," he says, "belongs to a clerkly class sitting on its arse, alone in studies and libraries, removed from any creative transformations of the material world."[2]

Memories return of my own lit crit days, shut away with some hard core critic in a cell of the library creatively transforming another's clever words into the latest collage which I would offer up in the hope of B (+). I also have in the back of my mind some old sepia film clips which record rather fish-faced students crowded into a theatrette while some glassy-eyed lecturer performs a kind of self-indulgent masturbation, with text in one hand and literary criticism in the other.

At first I was not much good at it. In the early days I wanted to say "I feel" and plunge straight into the text. But I persevered and practised the lit crit bit until I got it right. It began to be almost exciting. The year's rehearsals culminated in the multiple orgasm experience of the examination, where, in the space of three hours, I could usually finish off four essays. I did not come to love it but there were moments when, like the seasoned marijuana smoker, I almost came to perceive the pleasurable effects of what I was doing.

If I'd gone on to do a master's degree in the minor works of Joe Spriggs, who knows? I may even have reached the heights of sensitivity achieved by one of my lecturers, who, it is said, used to wake up all flushed after dreaming about the blurb on the dust jacket of the latest piece of R certificate literary criticism.

Most of the hard core stuff is not allowed into schools, of course, but it is amazing what can be achieved through the medium of the English essay, especially if the teacher stimulates the students by filtering through some of the choicer bits of literary opinion. Stimulation breeds emulation. Students come and students go but essays go on forever.

If you had put ten cents in a jar for every English essay you wrote at school and university, and were then to take ten cents out for every time you did it afterwards, how much money would be left in the jar by the time you were sixty?

Well, you can see that I have a few hang ups when it comes to universities.

Conversations

Doing English literature certainly had an unpleasant effect on my reading habits and it is only recently that I have begun again to enjoy the real thing; that is, responding to writers' meanings openly and generously.

Exhilarated at having thrown off my shame about those university days, I have been adopting the missionary position lately. When I have an audience, I want to convert them to the view that the urge to make stories, to listen to stories and to sing songs is natural for all of us. I want to argue that literature performs a basic social function. I want to convince English teachers and lecturers that reading literature is another form of conversation and that their role is to help the conversation along, not to write the script.

At a conference of Australian English teachers in 1974[3], I decided that I needed to make my point with authority, so I let blast with an impressive battery; Barthes, Eliot, Frye, Goldman, Mead, Trilling and Woolf, to name a few. I developed a complex conceptual model involving sets of interlocking triangles to illustrate the dialectic of literature and then set about showing that in a world which is in danger of running out of objective correlatives we need writers who can pump blood back into a constantly haemorrhaging language. Sartre and Proust were called to the bar to prove that the reader fills out the writer's work with his own meanings and that a work of art is nothing without a reader.

I also called on the linguists to give some new perspectives on the literary act by showing that literature is the only form of communication where "the language deliberately invites attention to itself",[4] that it is a "system of high cost information in which there is a novel use of arranged collocations".[5]

In full flight, I continued:

"Denied the paralinguistic aids of the spoken word, the gesture, the tone of voice, the pause and the volume control, the writer must somehow, through his knowledge of how words affect people, weave into his art form the gestural meanings which are immanent in speech."[6]

The applause at the end was gratifying. I came down from the rostrum, text in one hand and learned sources in the other. I looked steadily at my audience for the first time. They had the bemused look of voyeurs. I may have learnt the perils of lit crit but I still had not learnt to engage my audience in conversation.

But I must not ramble on. I know my arguments about the universities are likely to be as water-tight as a sieve. I just wanted to let you know that

I'm learning to read books again. I also wanted to tell you that in that talk back in 1974, I thought I knew best and loved talking about it. Now I know better and, having confessed it, I am relieved.

I have really enjoyed writing to you. Are you still with me? Or am I at it again?

Notes

1. Steiner, George. *Language and Silence.* Penguin, London, 1969.

2. Spriggs, Joe. "Doing Eng. Lit." in (ed) T. Pateman, *Counter Course.* Penguin, London. p. 228.

3. "Language as Literature", an address to the New South Wales English Teachers' Association, Sydney, 1974. A modified version of the talk appears in the E.T.A.Q. Newsletter, vol. 7, no. 4, November 1974.

4. 5. Phrases used in Barthes, Roland. *Mythologies.* Jonathan Cape, London, 1972.

6. See Gusdorf, Georges. *Speaking.* North Western University Press, Evanston, 1962.

Don't let anyone know your secret (or The language of universities) 13

I used to think that universities were deliberately designed to bamboozle students. I often think back to my own introduction to the university, Sydney University, and although I can laugh about it now, and even be cynical, it was traumatic at the time.

I remember, after the first week, trying to have my scholarship changed. I had looked at this impressive institute of learning, walked reverently along the path through the Quad, been reduced to silence by the library and had bowed in deference to the scholars. Then I went to see if I could change to the Teachers' College. But it was too late and my fate had been sealed. I thought then that I had been condemned to this institution for a period of four or more years. Now, of course, looking back, I am grateful that it wasn't quite so easy to escape.

Those first few weeks found me completely overawed. I was in a class of 1600 in Psychology I, and about the same number in English. And I was here to get an education. My ego had been well fed by winning the scholarship; it was bruised by my experience of the first few weeks.

To start with, I always felt inadequate. I always felt that I didn't know enough, wasn't intelligent enough, hadn't read enough. I was plunged into the "ignorant" category after having come from the "privileged" category of the secondary school. At school I had established a reputation for writing. I was used to having my essays greeted with praise and good marks. And I liked writing. I didn't confine myself to school writing but used to write for fun, relaxation and enjoyment. I was comfortable with words.

But that was before university English. I can remember my first lecture on John Donne. I'd read a lot of his poems, in school and out. I thought he was superb: he captured my imagination; I was excited by what he said to me. But that first lecture could have been about Sanskrit for all I understood. It was instant disillusionment. I had expected to go to the university to learn—but I had thought I would be able to understand the language!

73

There was a need for readjustment on my part. I wondered whether I hadn't understood Donne's poems when I had read them—or whether I couldn't understand the lecturer.

Being a seventeen year old fresher, I knew it must be me who was at fault. Why didn't I have more/better language so that I could comprehend what he was saying? Why was I so inadequate? I had pages of notes—but they didn't make sense. When I re-read the poems and tried to find what I was supposed to see, I just wasn't very clear about what I was looking for.

Where do you go for language when you haven't got it?

And it wasn't just Donne; the same thing happened to all the authors who were on my list. I began to think there was something drastically wrong with me. Why did I go to my lectures, having read the books, feeling reasonably comfortable about my ability to listen critically to a critic—and then come out so confused? Did I need to read more critics so I could understand criticism?

There were also the tutorials. I used to be so scared before them, that I would read everything that was recommended. I'd hope fervently that I wouldn't be asked a question. It's an awful pressure when you feel obliged to appear intelligent and learned.

I was aware that there was some sort of mystical language which I couldn't understand. The language of my lecturer and my tutor was not my language. Sometimes I had the feeling that I did know the answers to the questions which were being asked. I just couldn't sift through the questions quickly enough to find their meanings. At that stage of my life, intimidated by the language barriers to learning, I was convinced I was not good university material.

On one occasion there was a group of us swapping horror stories about the tutorial we had just endured and someone volunteered an interpretation of "that question" we had been asked. We were all dumbfounded. Is that *really* what he was asking, we demanded in unison? There was amazement and disbelief on the face of everyone present. We all knew the answer to that question—it was easy! Why couldn't he have said it in a way that we could have understood at the time.

When my first English assignment was returned, my inadequacies were reinforced. Twenty-six split infinitives? I may have been a good school essay writer but my teacher had not instructed me in the finer details. I didn't know about split infinitives. In my assignment on Jane Austen (one of my heroines, one of the first women to see clearly what was happening to women) there was no comment about meaning; no "feedback" on my contentious message. No, just twenty-six split infinitives!

After that I got my mother to teach me all the rules she knew, and she got out her old school Latin books to do it. We made this great list to hang above my desk so I could remember them all while I was writing. It was a great help, but it's hard to get involved in your writing when you have to check every sentence against a long list of rules. I didn't enjoy writing then!

I don't think they were particularly happy years in the lecture theatre and the examination hall, because they were always accompanied by a sense of frustration. I always felt that there was something just out of my reach, and if only I could take hold of it, everything would become meaningful. There was an elusive quality about my tertiary education. I passed, but without meaning.

There was never any depth to my understanding. There was rarely the satisfaction of something taken in and given my own meanings. In my third year, when any of my friendly authors were the lecture topics, I didn't go. It was easier that way. I could continue to read them, blissfully happy in my ignorance. I retained my own language, and rarely tried to mix it with my lecturer's. I kept my own voice for outside the university walls. It wasn't "good enough" on the premises.

By the time I enrolled for my master's degree, I wasn't so readily impressed any more. No longer seventeen, an undergraduate and ignorant, I was not plagued by the same feelings of inferiority. This may have been me; it may have been the lecturer who treated the seminar group of seven mature adults, in a manner much different from that of my tutor, many years before. Anyhow, for whatever the reason, I wasn't quite so willing to take refuge in being a simpleton. And I suppose this is where I think my "real" education started.

When a seminar was given — and I could not make sense of it — I said so. I had decided that if I didn't know the meaning of a word, it wasn't a very common word. And I was arrogant enough to think that if I couldn't understand what someone was saying, they weren't saying it very well!

In the fifteen minutes while the seminar leader explained what he was saying, I was enlightened. The props were set aside and there was a drab, uninteresting and unstimulating performance. I suddenly saw the language game. I had found that key which had tantalized me by being always just out of reach. I saw the speaker revealed without his covering coat of sophisticated jargon, and he looked very pale and insignificant. He had been hiding behind this complex, erudite language.

There was no need to be afraid of language any more. I wasn't so inferior. I had allowed myself to be mastered by the words of another. And now I wanted an explanation in my language. I wanted his voice, not his contrived and artificial paraphernalia. I discovered the marvellous power of challenging someone to say what he means. That's when the balance of power is reversed.

If you are going to allow yourself to be intimidated by language, then you must assume part of the responsibility. You cannot passively sit there and take it. Keep asking what "instructional episodes" really means, until someone says "lessons". Don't acquiesce to your own brow beating. Communication is a two-way process.

Start asking questions to find out how much of the complex language which is held up before you is necessary. Stop being bamboozled. I have found you can make it very awkward for posing people when you ask them what they mean.

Despite the fact that I am now quite capable of interrupting the learned, and saying, "I'm sorry, I don't understand", I find that so much of the language around me is pretentious. It is being used as a means of keeping people in their places. Lecturers constantly remind students of their lowly status through the use of complex language.

I am tired of listening to the simplest notions disguised so that only the pathologically determined are not deterred. I'm tired of language being used as an obstacle course to learning. I'm tired of one human being using language to prevent others from discovering what he knows, and calling the process "scholarship" and "excellence". I'm tired of the trappings of academia which coerce people into saying things in ways in which no-one else understands, because it is seen as a sign of intelligence and learning.

Language used to mystify is language misused. Language used to intimidate is abuse. Language used to keep people in their place is a blatant use of political power. Language used by educationists to keep people from knowing is a conspiracy. Language used to thwart learning in a tertiary institution is irresponsible.

And this is not just a plea of one who cannot cope — although there is an element of truth in it. I cringe when I hear a student seeking help with the meaning of a text and the response is:

> "Meaning is not just there you know. It has to be grappled with. You must wrestle with the words, fight with them if you are to gain meaning."

Why?

Language for learning is not the art of keeping people out, it is the art of drawing them in. Language, and making meanings, is not a battlefield. There is no virtue in jargon unless there are shared meanings present. It is crass ignorance to use jargon first and to defy the students to make meanings out of it. Jargon is a shorthand for which you need the meaningful symbols. It is a short circuit if you do not possess them. When there are meanings then jargon may follow!

There is only shallow achievement in leaving a lecture hall full of confused students. Status is not maintained by such perversity.

In a third year university course, the following lecture notes were dictated. Who can blame the students feeling cheated once they had deciphered its meaning.

> "Triadic activity is an activity of a person A, the teacher, the intent of whom is to bring about an activity, learning, by a person B, the pupil, the intention of whom is to achieve some end state (for example, knowing) whose object is X (for example belief, an attitude, a skill).
>
> There is a need for understanding the end achievement to which all is being directed.
>
> If the teacher is not clear what the end achievement the teacher is concerned with they can't know what is involved in B's learning X.
>
> Until they know what is involved in B's learning X they cannot know what is involved in A's teaching B X."

And this is not really jargon. It is just a string of convoluted sentences. This is not scholarship, or expertise. It is a pretence, and should be seen as such. It is using language to "dress up" simple concepts. It makes those who are in the "inferior" relationship to the teacher, conscious of this "inferiority". And who gains, who learns by such a process?

It is so simple, it is hardly worth saying, but it seems to be forgotten within tertiary confines. Say what you mean, and say it simply. The most intelligent person can adapt his language to be understood by his audience. There is no prize for being the only one who is capable of understanding; there is no prize for using language to keep the learner out!

14 Give up imitations, and try the real thing

Outlining the Parameters

I work in a university education department. Today I attended a colloquium (not entered in the Concise Oxford Dictionary, but bearing no resemblance to "colloquial") where I watched a student perform. He was a student I was supervising. Myself was at stake as well. We were both being measured.

In the few minutes which he took to say how he decided on his problems, I indulged in a "flashback" of the last few months. You see, I still have an image of myself as a teacher and I am not very secure in the Education Department. I spent years "out there" teaching English in comprehensive secondary schools, but that doesn't count for much here. I'm not very good at the new language; I can't speak fluently in research terms of methodology, conceptual framework, validity and reliability, and rotating the orthoganals. I still say method for strategy and plan for research design. I can't use the language of Phenix and I can't make many meanings out of the structure of knowledge.

But I have some expertise when it comes to kids and writing in schools. I have the empirical evidence of kids' writings, and I know what they are asked to write (and not to write). I've seen it. Countless examples of it. And I am concerned about it. And there was a student who came from the experiences of his practice teaching, who was also concerned. He'd seen the writing too (made empirical observations) and had decided that all was not well in the school (outlined the parameters of the problem).

So we talked about it (constructing the theoretical framework) and read what others had had to say (reviewing the literature) and looked at some of the kids' writings (the empirical evidence) and began to have some ideas (the conceptual framework). We realized that there were a number of questions (formulating the hypotheses) for which we had no answers.

- What *do* kids write in school?
- What sort of writing is it?
- Why do they write?
- Is it educationally justifiable?

Learning to Translate

And the student decided he wanted to know the answers (research study) and to tell others (thesis) but first he would have to let everyone know what it was he was trying to do (present a proposal at a colloquium).

That is where the trouble started I suppose. I was suddenly confronted with the task of translating my language into the required linguistic format of a thesis proposal. I had to get out of my words and develop the correct experimental orientation for an Education Department. I had not done anything like this before and I saw (perceived) it as my Achilles heel.

I had not acquired the experimentalists' linguistic table manners. I had not had the benefit of courses in research design and methodology. It was not my language and I was confused and intimidated by it. What I wanted to do, in my own language, was to look at the writing of students and ask why (insignificant problem).

We both felt vulnerable, but we were determined to imitate the voice that was necessary. We avidly read past proposals and quickly deduced the desired subheadings. We tried to make our meanings fit the prescribed form. We became anxious; we wrote and rewrote. We had days when we both became confused, when we lost our meanings in this foreign language, when we talked unintelligibly to each other — in the right words of course. Not that we ever lost sight of what we were trying to do; we just got entangled in the ways (which were not ours) of doing it. We were continually involved in translating; we would translate our language into that of research design and methodology, until we got lost in the process and had to translate back to the language which was close to us, to find out where we were. It was all very confusing — and time consuming.

During these uncomfortable sessions where we tried to find the correct formulae for our assessors, we often speculated on what it must be like to be a kid in school who was trying to write something to fit the teacher's format. We often wondered what it was like to be asked to be a kid who didn't have the same language as the teacher, but was required to write in the teacher's language. The students who were trying to imitate the teacher's voice had our deepest sympathy.

Linguistic Intolerance

It's almost an intelligence hurdle to say it the right way within the university. If you can't use the jargon, then the consensus is you have not got the idea (concept). There is linguistic intolerance abounding. There is pressure to be intiated into the linguistic rituals of the subject — and this means saying it the "right way". No one wants to appear a dummy on university premises, so there is a scramble for finding the accepted vocabulary. And that's what we did.

The proposal which the student presented represented an almost frenetic struggle to phrase his/our questions in someone else's language. And he had to sit there, at the head of the table, next to the chairman of the research committee, with members of the Education Department and other research students stretched out on either side, and he had to discuss his proposal.

I knew how he felt. It was much the same as I felt: nervous, vulnerable, exposed. The stated purpose of the exercise was for those present to provide him with constructive criticism. The role of the audience was to act as resources. He had the problem; they were going to help him make sure he had no other problems.

That was the intended learning outcome — but it wasn't what I learned, and I'll let him speak for himself. I learnt about intolerance. I learnt that there were some individuals present who were going to turn his problem into their problem; and there were some who thought that it was too insignificant to be a problem! (Insufficiently significant for an Honours Thesis proposal.)

If he had wanted to do a study on the teachers' perception of what kids write, or the student's perception of what teachers set, he would be working in educational psychology. If he had wanted to ascertain teachers' expectations of student writing, he would be working in educational sociology. He was working as an English educator; he wanted to look at children's writing.

He didn't want the evidence of the teacher's perception of the task, or the student's evaluation. He wanted the empirical evidence of the kid's writing.

They tried to take away the problem. They tried to turn it into something else; they tried to tell him and me we had no value. One individual leaving the colloquium stated with considerable condescension, "If something is not worth doing, it's not even worth doing well." He's in research, you know!

Why couldn't he keep his own voice? Why did they use a thesis to intimidate? Why did they try to change what he was saying? Why was there so much intolerance? Why were there so many parades of linguistic expertise?

I don't know the answers to this. Perhaps I learnt that only those who are insecure anyway try to imitate the voices of others. Perhaps I learnt I am my own worst enemy — that from the outset, the thesis proposal should have been written in the students' own language. Perhaps the fault lies in trying to play the game, and that education would be better served by being serious. But I hadn't been brave enough to try. I think I am now.

We have talked about it since, and have decided that it is futile to try and use someone else's language. If you want to make plain meanings, you should use your own. So that's how it's going to be written up.

The only question for which I have no answer now, and which worries me, is *will he pass?*

N.B. He did not complete the course!

15 A steaming heap of jargon: the language of the new education

Grass Roots

What is jargon? According to the Concise Oxford Dictionary it is "unintelligible words, gibberish; barbarous or debased language; a mode of speech full of unfamiliar terms."

Looking at the streams of "public service"/"education system" English that flow across my desk so often, I am struck not so much by the unfamiliarity of the terms (alas, they are all too familiar) as by the seeming ease and frequency with which they are used. Let me, by way of example, offer a little conglomerate that I have put together.

"To the D.G.E.

Attention: D.E.S. & R., A.D.S.E. and D.P.E.

Subject: Possible Changes in Methodology, Pedagogy and Instructology

At this point in time, we must consider the whole child in all his uniqueness, not by relying on the imposed curricula of the bureaucracy but rather by returning to the grass roots, to the coal face, to the cutting edge of education. The teacher not as teacher, but as facilitator or enabler, must cater for individualized needs by providing programmed learning sequences, uni-paks, super 8 cassette loading projectors and fully integrated, thematic and self-correcting modules. Above all, this personal growth and self-evaluated learning should proceed in open spaces, be conducted by teachers with open minds, using the open-book approach that will open new doors leading to the corridors of self-fulfilment.

It is by these methods that, in the realms of cognition, in the affective domain and in the skills area of sensory-motor co-ordination, the teachers of this day and age will nurture awakening minds, capable of withstanding future shock in the pluralistic society of tomorrow when technological advances will demand alternative education, deschooling and a return to the three R's.

Accordingly, I *recommend* that given the present circumstances, the case should be further investigated pending likely alterations to E.D. Circular 395, para 13a, since this is a matter of policy which could involve the setting of a precedent."

Now the shocking and, perhaps dangerous, revelation about the above piece is that it is not unfamiliar; nor is it entirely unintelligible. It does degenerate to gibberish from time to time but I'm sure that many of you have read or listened to similar language if you frequent the education scene. Some of you, like me, may have been guilty of using some of the phrases yourselves. It's so easy to do. Each year brings a new spate of "in" words which insidiously creep up on us and worm their way into our wordstore. Each conference seems to produce a fresh load of steaming jargon.

In our colleges and universities the sociologists, psychologists, psycholinguists and educationists weave a more and more sophisticated web of precise technical terms which the teaching profession and educational administrators seem only too ready to apply to anything.

What is wrong with the kind of language in my composite memorandum is that it can be so generally applied that it is empty of meaning. "Open", for instance, has become a word for all seasons although there was a time, no doubt, when it was used fairly precisely and with a great deal of effect. The mistake so often made by educationists is to "flog a dead horse"; the freshly minted and freshly meant word of today often becomes the debased coinage of tomorrow. Just consider what a flaccid and dreary word "creative" has become! How long before we begin to shudder at "grass-roots", "coal-face", "educational thrusts", "task forces" and "ad-hoc committees".

Word Swallowers

At one extreme we have the restricted language of the inner sanctum expert who is illiterate outside his specialty, at the other we have the uncritical or ecumenical word-swallower, so open-minded that his brains are likely to fall out. But it is not just terms that can throw us into fuzzy confusion. Some writers on education have developed complex sentence writing to a rare pitch of excellence. Lend your mind to this writer whose subject is communication!

"The unity and structure of the complete self reflects the unity and structure of the social process as a whole; and each of the elementary selves of which it is composed reflects the unity and structure of one of the various aspects of that process in which the individual is implicated."[1]

If I gather his meaning correctly, he is saying that we are influenced by and reflect the society in which we live.

Word Screens

One of our major tasks is surely to help our children and our educators to see through words to the meaning, or lack of meaning, behind them. Clever people can use words to bludgeon us, or to hypnotize us. The word screen is an effective weapon in modern society; it probably always has been. But it is not easy to sift out the worthy from the worthless. This does not mean that we should condemn the polysyllabic word out of hand.

We could become so anti-intellectual as to dismiss any speaker who uses words of more than two syllables. It is tempting for those of us with reluctant minds to shy away from new ideas just because of the language being used. Somehow, we've got to develop the ability to squeeze words to see if there is any substance. And, as I said before, many of the "in" words that we now deplore, can in the right context be used with great precision.

I suppose I'm coming around to the position that the fault lies not so much in the word as in the quality of thought that lies behind it.

Tauroballistics

Studying jargon can be fun. It's interesting to contemplate how certain words, like dirty jokes, catch on and go the rounds. There is a real fascination in considering the history of educational jargon in South Australia. You only have to read the Director's Report of 1906 to realize that educators have always had a patent on a special brand of jargon, or should we say tauroballistics (the art of bull-shooting).

> "The character of its inspectorial staff is vital to the well-being of any system of education, no matter how adequately the system fulfils, in other respects, approved theoretical principles. It may, indeed, be said that as is the inspector so is the system. . . . Professional work of any sort tends to narrow the mind and limit the point of view, and to put a hallmark on a man of a most unmistakable kind, and the inspector who is to prove 'an influence in his district must fight strenuously against such tendencies. To set others aglow he must keep his own fires burning. How shall *he* give kindling in whose inward man there is no live coal, but all is burnt out to a dead, grammatical cinder?'."

A STEAMING HEAP OF JARGON 85

Turning the Sods

It is also fun to ring the changes on jargon. A senior administrator was recently opening an inservice conference attended by a group of bright-eyed young teachers. Part of his text went like this:

> "You have all heard of the grass roots approach to educational problems. But I would like to say that the only trouble with the grass roots is that they never see the light. So what is needed occasionally is someone to come along with a ruddy great shovel and turn the sods over."

Permanent Space Dividers

Wherever there are new movements and new ideas in education, inevitably new words are coined to help map out the new domain. This is nowhere more apparent than in the areas of open education and assessment (or evaluation). I sometimes think that those teachers privileged to be teaching in open units have deliberately built up a house of words to keep the barbarians outside the gates in awe and reverence (and in a suitable state of mystification).

The new equipment alone has produced some beauties like "portable trapezoidal tables" and "modular visual barriers". Then we have "withdrawal areas", "individualized instruction posts" and "optional electives". One school I heard about recently has decided that it wants to return to traditional classrooms and so it has requisitioned for walls under the guise of "permanent space dividers".

Some of the more seasoned teachers can be excused a certain amount of cynicism when they see an excess of fuss being made about what are essentially very simple but fundamental ideas. It will be a pity if the ideals of "open education" fall into disrepute because teachers, entranced with the technology and the lingo, lose sight of children.

At the centre of the open education movement on a world scale you will find not luxuriously appointed "open units" but rather a core of concerned teachers with deeply held convictions which might go something like this:

- All human beings should be valued equally.
- Children are born into the world as inquirers and will continue to inquire given the right conditions.
- Education should be based on human understanding and affection.
- Because people are different as much choice as possible should be offered in schools.

Now these beliefs have no direct connection with certain styles of educational architecture nor with the accompanying pseudo-technical language of "open" education. They can be put into practice in any school where the teachers share such convictions.

My point is that to give over the limelight and the brass bands to new architecture and new technologies is to risk obscuring the true goals of education.

Symbol Magic

Getting back to my earlier point, I am saying, in other words, that all of us must be on our guard to see that language is not used to divert people from reality, nor to coerce the gullible, nor to bewilder the naive.

An area of crucial significance here is the very language which the school values as an institution, and its relationship with the language of the community. What may be perceived as perfectly standard, acceptable and clear English by the teachers in the school, may be indeed alien, or mystifying, or exclusive to the "average" citizen.

The official communications from school to parents may be perceived as jargon by many people and this may have profound implications. For instance, the notion of school as a threatening "different" and "elitist" institution could be dramatically reinforced by the language face which the school turns to its community (and for that matter, to its students).

Assessments and school reporting concern me particularly. How often do we hoodwink our clients with carefully obscure reporting which pays lip service to obligations while in effect fobbing parents off with "symbol magic"?

> "Johnny is inclined to be talkative but we have noted a pleasing improvement in Mathematics. B+."

If the school often unwittingly holds the community at bay with language, there is no doubting also that the educational researchers and professional quoters of research are most adept at keeping teachers at bay and making them feel inferior.

Rigor Mortis

But let's not stop at educators in naming the groups who excel in wielding language as a weapon to subjugate, humiliate and mystify. I've known medical practitioners who were past masters at holding the patient in a state of panic while they peddled their deliberately non-committal diagnosis couched in deliberately vague terms. The lawyers seem to delight in keeping the masses in ignorance, weaving their abstruse Latinate contracts, their affidavits and their summonses, in the name of absolute clarity. Similarly, one could name advertising agencies, politicians, police officers and parking inspectors—all have been known to hold their own humanity in check, by hiding behind a wall of words.

In the light of the above, I would conclude, and I hope you might support me, that at the very heart of our attempts to provide a better education for our children should be education in language, education against language empires and education towards clear thoughts in warm and living words. Jargon is the first sign of impending rigor mortis.

Notes

1. Moffet, James. *Teaching the Universe of Discourse.* Houghton Mifflin, N.Y., 1968, p. 66.

16 Have you thought about sex lately?

"It is an educational disadvantage to be a girl"

So, we've had International Women's Year and there is just too much fuss being made about sex! The whole issue is out of perspective. Of course, there are a few things where perhaps women aren't getting a fair deal, but even they are going quickly. But it's gone too far. Everyone knows that it's not nearly as bad as some of these angry women would have us think!

Your sentiments perhaps? Your carefully determined assessment of the situation?

If it is, then I think that it needs challenging. There are a number of questions which I would like to ask, and I don't pretend to have the answers (though I'm prepared to make an "educated guess" in some instances). But before I ask the questions it would probably be quite good tactics to dispense some comforting words, designed to put you at ease, so that you don't feel defensive from the outset. I have something serious to say and I would rather not allow you the opportunity to rationalize your way out of it. I don't want you to be able to dismiss me as a wild and raging women's libber. That would be too easy. Because I want you to face the issues I am raising, I am going to try and prevent you from dismissing me on emotional grounds.

This is no platform for "Women's Liberation"; no screeching or neurotic tirade against the male oppressor. It is an important argument with strict educational parameters, and one which demands serious attention. There is an analogy.

If I were to say that lower class children were being denied full and open access to education in the average "middle class" school, I would expect due attention to be paid to my evidence for this statement. That my statement is lifted straight from the Karmel Report — "it is an educational disadvantage to be a girl" — is an argument which has its origins in the inability of one section of the population to gain full and open access to knowledge. It is equally deserving of serious consideration as the statement about "lower class" children.

If education is to provide students with the means to realize their full potential, then any action which limits or reduces the scope of that potential is anti-educational in spirit. If a teacher adopts a position which either deliberately or unintentionally restricts the horizon of the student, on the basis of the teacher's assumptions and definitions of sex, then the teacher is doing the student a disservice. That "everyone knows" that the two sexes are different, is insufficient validation for the practices of some teachers or the policies which inform some schools.

Male chauvinism or improvisation? — Sex object or agricultural implement?

Sexism

The word that is used to delineate this phenomenon in action is *sexism*, and it describes a specific way of looking at the world (in the same way as racism does). Its functioning is probably "automatic" for many individuals, as its values are institutionalized, and may never have been questioned. If you are serious about education, teaching and kids, then perhaps you should know more about *sexism*.

> "SEXISM (n). (1) a belief that the human sexes have a distinctive make up that determines their respective lives, usually involving the idea that one sex is superior and has the right to rule the other. (2) a policy of enforcing such asserted right. (3) a system of government and society based on it."[1]

Because the values implicit in sexism are institutionalized, then any questioning of them is a direct challenge to the status quo. But in an educational framework where:

- females leave school before males,
- where they leave in possession of different skills,
- where fewer females attend university, and
- where females occupy few of the top jobs,

the status quo deserves challenging. Perhaps the answer will be that females have less ability than males, or perhaps they have different functions, or perhaps they are fulfilled in different ways. If these are the answers, then the questions will have been dealt with satisfactorily, and there is an end to it. But if, and this is why the exercise is worthwhile and serious, it is because of some of the unfounded assumptions which are present in the minds of individuals in society, and these are perpetuated in schools, then perhaps it is time to change those assumptions.

In this educational context, the cliche cannot count as hard data. There is no room in an educational debate for "everyone knows". There is a need to rise above the emotional outburst and to attempt to verify — or refute — some of the beliefs which determine educational practices.

It is common knowledge that females do not achieve the same things, or to the same degree as males do. This is no evidence for anything. The evidence lies in the answer to why don't females do as well as males. Because females do not go on to tertiary education in the same numbers as males, is the starting point, *not the conclusion!* It is necessary to start with what is known, to determine whether this superiority of the male in educational terms is real or apparent. And if the emperor doesn't have any clothes, then there is a responsibility to admit it. There is nothing, emotional, extremist, aggressive or neurotic, if you state that the emperor is without apparel.

To question sexism as it functions within the curriculum in the school is to question most school activities. For the sake of convenience (and at the risk of being regarded as illogical) the following areas have been chosen to be illustrative and representative of some of the sexist bias which underlies education.

- Inequality of access to knowledge
- Subject-Content area
- The hidden curriculum
- Reduced expectation
- Career

Inequality of Access to Knowledge

There have been numerous efforts made in the past to ensure equal educational opportunity for all children. It is still debatable whether such a goal has been achieved, but at least educators were aware that not all children possessed equality of opportunity and they directed their efforts towards eliminating and minimizing the inequalities.

Are we aware that the way in which our schools operate today precludes the access of some students to knowledge? Are we aware that we deliberately stop some people from finding out about certain things, based on the assumptions that:

- girls need to be taught to cook
- girls are homemakers
- sewing is important for girls
- girls don't "need" certain subjects
- girls can't "do" certain subjects

School electives and timetables are designed to "slot" girls into the "domestic subjects" based on an assumption that girls need to be "domestics". (I know of few schools where fathercraft, home handyman, and household maintenance are taught—though this would be just as indefensible if not open to both sexes.) If girls wish to do metalwork it is considered to be an eccentric request in some schools, and the victim is treated accordingly.

Girls can be denied access to vast areas of science (where girls' schools notoriously opt for the "softer" biology instead of the "harder" physics and chemistry). This is only a superficial glance at the practices of the schools. Assumptions are constantly being made as to what girls can and cannot do, should and should not do and when these assumptions are those of the policy makers and school administrators, the scope of education for females is being curtailed. Someone is keeping them out.

Yet in other areas, so many allowances are made for individual differences. Gross generalizations about ability and interest for 51 per cent of the population on any basis other than sex, would be the object of immediate query. For example, if 51 per cent of the students in a school were considered to be working class, and those in authority assumed that working class children did not like/need/appreciate good literature, and therefore should not have it, how long would it be before someone started to ask awkward questions? How long before someone speculated that perhaps the reason such children did not respond positively to good literature was because they were unfamiliar with it? How long before there was an argument for even greater justification for giving them good literature?

How long before we decide that therefore girls need greater access to physics and chemistry? Why is it that sex imposes limits, but that other debilitating factors such as different culture or class, present challenges? The next time someone says that males are better at mathematics and science than females, have a look at the emperor's clothes.

Subject-Content Area

At school I was a history student. I like history. Once I learned that Mrs Pankhurst chained herself to a rail. I thought she was a bit extreme.

At university I was a history student. I spent one whole year studying nineteenth century history. I admit, I wasn't a model student, I did not scavenge through the library looking for books, but I did manage to read most of the books which the lecturer recommended.

I studied nineteenth century history and I did not find out during the whole year that one of the big issues of the nineteenth century was women's rights. Who writes these books?

> "The woman-problem had become one of the most earth shaking debates of the western world. Even in countries where the feminist situation was minor or non-existent, the great question nevertheless provoked outraged concern. Tolstoy, in a Russia nearly untouched by feminism, had to be as worried about keeping women in their place as England's William Gladstone. The 'woman-problem' was argued about, raved about, agonized about endlessly, endlessly. One would be hard pressed to find any major figures of the period in any cultural field who did not address themselves passionately to the rights of women. As for lesser figures . . . the amount of literature (newspapers, magazines, novels, dramas, scholarship, pamphlets) that emerged from the ranks of now forgotten feminists and anti-feminists must surely outweigh the material we have on any other social issue of modern times."[2]

I want to know where all this material went. Why didn't I find out about it when I did history? Who chose what "history" was and on what basis? And is it any better today?

> "Ask most high school students who Jane Adams, Ida Tarbell or Susan B. Anthony were and you may get an answer. Ask about Margaret Sanger, Abigail Dunaway, or Margaret Brent and you probably get puzzled looks. Soujourner Truth, Francis Wright, Anna Howard Shaw, Emma Willard, Mary Biekerdyke, Maria Mitchell and Providence Crandall and scores of others sound like answers from

some historians' view of trivia. Interest in the fate of obscure Americans may seem an esoteric pursuit, but this is not the case. History, despite its enviable reputation for presenting the important facts about the past, is influenced by considerations other than the simple love of truth. It is an instrument of the greatest social utility, and the story of our past is a potent means of transmitting cultural images and stereotypes."[3]

After I ceased being a history student, I suddenly found this whole new area of nineteenth century history, and a mass of information about women. Why had the doors of this subject been closed to me during my formal education?

The next time someone tells me that:

- women have made no contribution to history,
- that there are no great women in history,
- that women are not fit historical subjects,

I am going to ask where his clothes are. I think the emperor is expecting too much!

But what about the other subjects? Is history the only sexist subject? What about English for example. Surely no such savage prejudice operated in the liberal area of English. There are some good female novelists!

I've looked at our literary heritage and I've seen Jane Austen and George Eliot. But I have asked why so many of the female novelists submitted their manuscripts to the publishers with male pseudonyms? Is it that:

- There are more/better male writers?
- There were just as many/more/better female writers, but *they didn't get published*?
- Jane Austen, George Eliot and the Brontes were an accident? Did some unsuspecting publisher think they were men, until too late?

There has recently been a book published which is guaranteed to challenge the most entrenched sexist bias. It is not a book of propaganda; it is a collection of unpublished manuscripts, across six centuries, written by women. These writings have played no part in our literary heritage; there has been no public access to them. They are not writers who have been studied traditionally in the educational context. They are the writings of gifted women — and like the history of women, I didn't know they existed until 1974.

Is there a literary heritage hidden from common view, composed by women? What has happened to the women who have written down through the ages?

> "Did I my lines intend for public view
> How many centuries would their faults pursue.
> Some would, because such words they do affect,
> Cry they insipid, empty, incorrect.
> And many, have attained, dull and untaught
> The name of wit, only by finding fault.
> True judges, might condemn their want of wit
> And all might say, THEY'RE BY A WOMAN WRITT
> Alas! A woman that attempts the pen
> SUCH AN INTRUDER ON THE RIGHTS OF MEN."[4]

But things have changed, I hear you say, that doesn't happen any more! Doesn't it?

> ". . . the world will slight her . . . who rather makes odes than beds.
> Lost Lady! Gentle fighter!
> Separate in time, we mutiny together."[5]

Although most university English graduates confess to many tedious hours wrestling with a minor Victorian poet, they may never have heard of Anne Finch. Aphra Behn, a brilliant writer, is not listed among their classics. They have been denied the insights of Olive Schreiner, the challenges of Arias Vin and the stimulation of Dilys Laing. And how many more were there?

The English curriculum represents an accumulated-over-the-years sexist bias. It is a collage of male choices of male literature, with a few mishaps on the way. Where have all the women gone? Well you might ask; ask the emperor!

And what about anthropology, and philosophy and psychology? Could we scratch the surface of those mainly male enclaves, and find the same things underneath? Would it be found again and again that sexism has pervaded the content of these areas, in the same way that it has determined historical content and literary heritage? If the content we teach as teachers is biased, do we have an obligation to point out this fact to our students?

The Hidden Curriculum

Within the classroom, there are many things which are taught and learned beyond the specified content area. These are incidental learnings and are referred to as the "hidden curriculum", as distinct from the intentional learnings provided for by the curriculum. What do teachers teach students besides the actual content area of their subjects?

What definitions of male and female, of young lady and young man, determine the teacher's attitudes towards the students? What do kids learn, even from pre-school, when the teacher asks the boys to put the furniture back into place, and the girls to clean up? What do they learn when we make English (reading and writing) a passive activity? When do they learn that girls are "better" at English and that only sissies like poetry?

Do we start to make them masculine and feminine when we make girls wear skirts as school uniforms (limited action possibilities) and boys wear trousers (much more freedom)? What are they learning when we tell little girls that it is not nice to be aggressive, and little boys to stand on their own two feet, and that only little girls cry? What do they learn when we read them stories in which women are "stupid", "passive", "dependent" and in which men are "intelligent", "active" and "independent"?

What do they learn when we punish boys by making them sit with the girls? What do they learn when boys are caned and girls get lines? What do they learn when teachers tolerantly accept boys scuffling in the classroom but find comparable behaviour from girls cause for severe punishment? What do they learn when all the important positions in the school are occupied by men? What do they learn from the way teachers, male and female, interact with one another? What sort of models do the teachers provide?

When they open their textbooks and find that boys become prime ministers and girls become first ladies, that boys invent things and girls use them, and that boys have careers and girls have families, what are they learning? When they see a picture of a smiling, feminine Madame Curie resting her hand on the shoulder of a busy male who is peering down a microscope, what do they learn? When there is either a different novel for boys and for girls, or the reading materials provided are more exciting when they depict the lives of boys, what do they think about themselves?

So boys conform to the masculine model, and girls conform to the feminine model. The only argument that this substantiates is that they are being well taught. But why are they being taught these things? Either we should start saying that the emperor has no clothes—or that those of the empress are identical. There doesn't seem to be any reason for continuing with the argument that the emperor is better dressed.

Reduced Expectations

Recently a teacher entered a new senior mathematics class and asked the girls who were present what they were doing there. A science master advised some girls to do biology.... "because they would find it easier". A young English teacher advised her class of girls to be discreet in the ways in which they aired their knowledge in front of men, because most men were uncomfortable with women who were "intellectually challenging". A mathematics teacher offered the platitude that it wasn't important for the girls to understand a particular concept because they would never need it.

All these are examples of teachers holding reduced expectations of girls. Teachers do not expect them to do as well as boys, or, if they do, not to show it. Teachers rarely expect that education and a career is as important to a girl as it is to a boy. The assumption in many schools is that the business of education for males is to fit them for a career; for females it is to fit them for homemaker.

What would be incredible would be if more of them rejected the roles which their education delineates for them. What would be amazing would be the progress of more females towards access to the status positions in society. What is unfortunate is that in this sense, education works. Females fulfil the reduced expectations that are operating for them.

> "It must be made clear that the high school woman does not learn that she should be an idiot. Rather the message is 'Don't be *too* smart or *too* successful.' As Margaret Mead comments, '. . . throughout her education and her development of educational expectancy, the girl is faced with the dilemma that she must display enough of her abilities to be considered successful, but not too successful . . .' The goal is to avoid either extreme and find that perfectly uncontroversial level of mediocrity."[6]

Is it an educational disadvantage to be a girl, because education is designed to disadvantage girls? And what about the converse? Is education fair or is it one of the most powerful ways of preventing people from seeing that the emperor has no clothes?

Career

It would be interesting to confront a group of male students and to ask them whether they saw any conflict between career and fatherhood.

> "Do you think that you will be able to fulfil the two roles successfully? Do you think there is any conflict between having a career and having children? Do you think you will be depriving your children in any way?"

If I then added that there were a number of occupations which were suitable for combining the two roles, such as teaching, because of the school holidays, I wonder how free the males would feel to choose a career?

When being counselled for a career, how many girls who say they are considering nursing are asked whether they would like to be a doctor?

What do careers counsellors say to girls who express interest in engineering? That boys might want a career that keeps them outside is readily accepted. What happens when a girl conveys similar values?

It is not only that girls are not given the same range of careers to choose from, they are also burdened with the notion that it is not a free choice. There are few fifteen year olds in the process of making choices about their future who are brave enough to go against the mores. There is pressure to be successful "females" which means, translated, to say that the emperor's clothes are really very nice. It is too much to expect that they will state that he doesn't wear any.

So have a think about sex and equality, and be amazed that women do so well given so many handicaps. The educational disadvantage of being a girl lies in the education. Perhaps it is in need of change.

Notes

1. Shortridge, Kathleen. "Women as University Nigger" in Ann Arbor, *University of Michigan Daily Magazine.* 12 April, 1970.

2. Roszak, Theodore. "The Hard and the Soft" in Roszak, T. and Roszak, B. (ed) *Masculine/Feminine.* Harper Colophon, New York, 1969, p. 88.

3. Trecker, Janice. "Women in U.S. History Textbooks", in *Social Education*, 35, No. 3, March, 1971.

4. Goulianos, J. (ed). *By a Woman Writt.* Penguin, Maryland. 1973.

5. From Mead, Margaret, *Male and Female,* William Morrow, New York. 1949, p. 320.

6. Frazier, Nancy, and Sadker, Myra. *Sexism in School and Society.* Harper & Row, N.Y., 1973, p. 320.

17 *It's all done with mirrors*

Through the Looking Glass

Mirrors are magic. They can reflect, distort, exaggerate, diminish and turn everything upside down. As a child, walking through the Hall of Mirrors, I was easily convinced that there was no limit to their power. Mirrors could change everything around so that you could no longer recognize reality. Mirrors could make sure that what you saw wasn't true. Mirrors were a window on the absurd, as Alice found out when she went through the looking glass.

Whenever I was confronted with something which just would not make sense, I could, as a last resort, dismiss it with a nonchalant shrug and say "Aha, it is all done with mirrors." When things appeared to be topsy turvy, and there seemed no reasonable rationale, the mirror trick always came in handy. It made me feel secure because I could ignore those things which just wouldn't add up; I could say they weren't real. There was no need for me to be confused.

I have reason to be grateful to the mirror. I became a teacher. I found so much that was topsy turvy, so much that was upside down and back to front, that I was in daily need of the mirror. I had to call on it constantly to make sense of the educational world. If I had not been able to say with relief, "It is all done with mirrors", then I'm sure I should have just wandered aimlessly through its bewildering paradoxes.

To me, education means first of all people. People who want to know about things; who want to explore and find out. Teaching means providing those people with access to the things they want and need to know. That is a simple and common sense approach to schooling. Take what the students have, stimulate them with a wide variety of experiences and then help them to answer their own questions.

Before I went teaching I had no idea that education was first of all the art of preventing students from asking questions, and secondly, to prevent them from finding any answers. I can only presume that I was naive and innocent.

Keep it to Yourself

Recently I was talking to a teacher who had a composite class of Grade Three and Grade Six. "Marvellous", I said envisaging the advantages of having the older students involved with the younger students. A stimulating and enriching experience for all. "Dreadful," she retorted acidly, declaring how it was almost an impossible task to keep the two grades separated. She revealed that she was constantly plagued by the fear that Grade Six would "tell all" to Grade Three and then she'd be in a mess with the syllabus. The children in her class lived with the threat of harsh penalties if she caught them "mixing". It would be outrageous behaviour for a Grade Six child to assist a Grade Three child with his work. They must not, under any circumstances, be told the answers.

If, like me, you think education is all about providing answers then, like me, you would be very grateful to the mirror. I couldn't make sense of the education this teacher was offering her students. I had to say it was all done with mirrors.

But she was no unique exception, this teacher. No, if anything, I am the outsider. There are many who share her view of the world.

Faced with a primary class, I encountered a little boy who was sitting glumly with the letters of the alphabet scattered around him. They were all jumbled up, and obviously were meaningless symbols to him. The teacher said that he had been sitting there with them every morning, and still he did not know them.

Within the same class, I noticed a bright perky little girl, eager to share her knowledge with anyone who would listen, and restless because she was forced to sit through the repetitious practices of a spelling lesson — on words she could spell effortlessly. She had however been prohibited from going on to the next list because the class wasn't ready yet. Thinking perhaps that the problems of two children in the class might be solved, I suggested to the teacher that the little girl go and help the little boy with his alphabet.

Obviously, it was some form of heresy which I proposed: my suggestion was met with a vehement reply. "How ridiculous" she admonished me. "She would only tell him the answers."

That was exactly what he needed. The answers. Sitting there surrounded by a series of questions — which and what and how, he desperately needed someone to tell him the answers. But that teacher was going to stop him from getting them.

School would be one of the few places where co-operation is called cheating. It's because the premise underlying schooling is that if you know something, keep it to yourself. Don't tell anyone the answers.

And if you don't believe me, go and ask any teachers if you can borrow their most successful programs. Most of them won't lend them. They don't want you to know. They will jealously guard their knowledge.

If it's not a trick with mirrors, what is it?

Think about examinations. I was once asked to teach a series of six lessons on a most horrific topic to a class of thirteen year olds. I protested that it was ludicrous to even commence such a task, I was sternly admonished and told I would have to. There was a question on the topic in the examination.

I checked out the examination paper and decided that I could teach the students the answer in one lesson, so I approached the teacher again, proposing that I spend five lessons teaching something more appropriate. In the sixth lesson I would teach the students the answer for the examination. Besides, I could be sure that they would "learn" it, if I treated it that way.

The teacher concerned became hysterical. My suggestion was absolutely unthinkable. When I asked why it was educationally more sound to teach the topic over six lessons, and to hide the clues and right answers for the exam, than it was to teach it in one, I must admit he was at a loss for words.

I should have thought that if one of the purposes of teaching the topic was for regurgitation in the examination, then to take one lesson instead of six was considerably more efficient. I could not see how the material was enhanced by hiding the examination answer within it. I knew if I told the students the sixth lesson would contain the answer for the exam they would all be most attentive.

When I tried to give the students the answer the school said they needed, I was called into the headmaster's office for disciplining. He informed me that if I was going to survive as a teacher I'd have to learn pretty quickly that you didn't go round giving students the answers.

What do you give them then? I don't understand. It has to be all done with mirrors.

It Can't Really be True

I started to listen to the staff room conversation around me. I was becoming increasingly bewildered. "My students can't write so I'm going to give them writing every day this year." How often have you heard it? Be it mathematics, or French vocabulary or historical facts. If you can't do something, what is the educational point of finding out every day that you can't do it? It could hardly be called constructive. If a child could not play football and was forced by a parent to play it every day, on the basis that he could not play it, then you'd have to say the parent was misguided and cruel. And you would have to expect that the child would come to loathe football (and perhaps his parent as well), he would in all probability begin to feel a failure, and he, would be quite likely to develop a host of other complexes as well.

Yet when teachers use this argument, with regard to education, it is accepted as reasonable and sound. To me, it is a foolish and absurd argument. The only way I can live with it is to call it a distortion of the mirror. It can't really be true.

An English subject master was recently asked by a member of his staff if the students could attend a visiting performance of a rare and stimulating Australian play. He judged the request unreasonable because the students had "done" the play and answered the examination question on it. There was nothing to justify their attendance at the performance. I wonder if he also thought the play had been written with the examination question in mind?

Think of all the familiar distorted and nonsensical arguments that you hear in schools every day:

- "I don't care if it means you will never want to read another novel again, you'll answer questions on every chapter of this one."
- "All students who borrow books from the library, have to write a book review and hand it in when they return the book." That one is easy. You stop borrowing library books.

- "There's not time to answer questions, you'll just have to listen to what I have to say."
- "There will be no talking in my classroom."
- "I don't care if you don't understand it. Learn it!"
- "I know they'll forget it as soon as the exam is over, but they won't need it then."

This is the common currency of education. It is upside down, back to front, absurd and ludicrous. It is a system which has lost sight of reason. It is not education at all. It is a trick of the mirror.

Advising a young teacher on the teaching of the novel, a wise and experienced teacher warned against the practice of telling the students anything interesting. This was a fatal mistake, because it was all they remembered when it came to the examination. They didn't put the real things in their answers.

While I was still puzzling over what the real things were, as distinct from the interesting things, another teacher came forward with his solution to the problem. He told the students the interesting things, but he threatened them with all manner of dire circumstances if they dared to mention them in the examination. He concluded that his method was efficient because "no-one ever wrote anything interesting in their exam essays".

If it's not mirrors, what is it? It cannot be reality.

And it's easy to see how the young, enthusiastic and eager teachers are overwhelmed and confused when they enter the educational realm of Catch 22. Mistakenly thinking that they are there to ask questions and help students find answers, they soon begin to wonder what is going on in the upside down school.

When student teachers are told by supervising teachers that kids are the enemy and that the teachers' task is to get on top of them, it is no wonder that they find the school an inhospitable place. You cannot blame them for their amazement when they are told by the headmaster that he will not support them if they do anything which can be interpreted as being "friendly" to the students.

Don't Talk to Them

What must be the educational philosophy behind this package of advice which was delivered to a group of final year practice teachers?

- Don't give them homework, because they won't do it.
- Don't ask them questions, because they don't know how to answer.
- Don't give them anything interesting, because they get excited.
- You can always tell when a class is going off to an "easy" teacher. They look as though they are about to enjoy themselves.

- Don't try and be reasonable with them, they just don't understand.
- They can't think. They can only copy from the board.

How can these student teachers reconcile this advice with the valuable ideas they have come into contact with in the university ivory tower? No wonder so many of them want to leave before they have ever really begun.

But one teacher must win the prize for the mirror trick. Taking the student teacher aside, he proceeded to deliver the essence of educational wisdom.

"If you want to get on", he said, "just *don't talk to them*. Just go in and fill the board with notes. So many that they have to go like fury to try and get them all copied down in the lesson. And watch out for the smart ones who leave out a line. They'll try and tell you they didn't notice. That's the only way to handle them. And you can always prove you've done your job that way. Their books are always full of notes."

When the student teachers who become victims of this warped educational philosophy ask me for an explanation, I can only reply that it's all done with mirrors. But we cannot afford this distortion and inversion indefinitely. The mirrors will have to go. Soon, even the mirror, powerful as it is, must shatter under the strain!

18 *The sociolinguistic interface*

"On behalf of the Captain and the crew I should like to welcome you aboard and to wish you a pleasant flight . . . and you are reminded that smoking in the toilet is strictly prohibited."

I didn't really listen. We were being painlessly elocuted by a graduate of the school of good grooming where vowels are delicately choreographed and the text is precisely intoned according to the established hymnal.

Have you ever thought what the hosties mutter to each other when the coffee is spilled in the galley? Do they swear in impeccable hostessese?

* * *

We were soon aloft, on our way from Adelaide to Alice Springs. I'd brought along a spectrum of reading materials and I was soon ploughing into Michael Halliday's *Explorations of the Functions of Language* (Edward Arnold, 1973).

It was difficult to understand why he places so much emphasis on the crucial sociolinguistic interface of language. Indeed, it was difficult to understand what he means by the "sociolinguistic interface". I thought that it must have something to do with people from different classes, or different socio-economic circumstances or different cultures rubbing up against each other with their languages.

I wondered whether any of it applied in Australia where, they will tell you, most of us speak the same lingo and Jack is as good as his master in a paradise of egalitarianism.

My reverie was interrupted by coffee, a couple of biscuits and the aroma of the hot meals coming from the first class section.

Far below lay Lake Eyre, gorged with water, vast and blue. It was so restful that I gave up trying to fathom what Halliday could mean and I turned instead to Flaubert, Madam Bovary and her dull-witted husband who, after failing first time round, finally made it through medical school.

"So Charles set to work again and crammed for his examination, ceaselessly learning all the old questions by heart. He passed pretty well. What a happy day for his mother." (Chapter 1)

The sky was now clear and it was not long before we swept into the Alice airport with the Macdonnells on our left and wintery Adelaide somewhere on our right.

Max and Jane, representing the tourist association, were there to meet us and guided us to a battered old Bedford liberally coated with the red dust of the dead heart.

As we trundled off towards the gap and the Alice, Max, cowhide-skinned and impressively unkempt, introduced himself.

"Like to welcome you all to the Alice. My name's Max. I'm bloody mad but wait till you see the rest of the drivers. Anyhow, relax and enjoy it . . ."

* * *

I looked around at my fellow tourists and put on some imaginary labels — the adventurous university student; the ancient English couple on a world tour; two Sydney "housewives" about to live it up; a couple of retired couples, well-to-do; the foreign girl and her Australian chaperone; the lonely middle aged introvert trying to conceal his fastidiousness . . .

Max had set them all at ease. His vulgarity was "right". We were now in a Disney kind of adventureland where the bus driver was the hard-bitten hero who'd seen it all. He transcended class barriers.

So the laconic Max kept us informed and entertained past every landmark, like the drive-in "where fifty percent went to watch the pictures", and the "Abo's detoxification tents" ("and by the way I can tell you that what you hear down south about racial strife is bullshit, if you don't mind me saying so . . . but I wouldn't advise you to drink in the front bar of the Alice Springs Hotel").

* * *

After settling in at the motel we went for a Saturday walk down the main street, taking in the dustiness and the empty beer cans and the small clumps of Aborigines in their ill-worn uniforms, the floppy floral dress, the check shirt and the grubby jeans.

Later that night we called in for a drink at the Stuart Arms Hotel Saloon Bar. Not an Aborigine in sight. The management has nothing against Aborigines. They simply exclude unacceptable uniforms. "Strictly no T-shirts, jeans and thongs" said the notice, obviously meant for white people . . . because they can read.

* * *

The next day the tourist bus rolled up with a new driver, Geoff, a smoother version of Max with a slightly more sophisticated patter. But he still looked like a Central Australian in his khaki clobber, his tan necktie and his budding gut—probably allied to a redness around the gills which could not be attributed entirely to the sun.

He too set us at ease with his racy lingo, bordering on the crude. In fact he proved to be a master of public relations, with a language for all occasions.

He soon had us happily chattering to each other with dymo tape Christian names tags pinned on our chests. The labels worked like magic as we jolted over the red corrugations.

Fifty odd kilometres out he stopped to let us have a look at the "wildflowers".

"You might like to 'ave a bit of a stagger. Gents to the right, ladies to the left. No hurry, we've got mobs of time."

Thanks to the labels, I managed to have a good conversation over the wildflowers.

When we returned, Geoff hoped we felt "more better" and reminded the "birds" that since this was International Women's Year they should feel quite free to "chat him up".

The Domino Theory

Pinter would have been in his element at the Mission.

Buckboards full of listless Aborigines bounced seemingly without aim around the dusty settlement, while peaceful looking lotus eaters sat in motley groups considering I know not what. Kids ran around kicking up the dust.

Matthew, our Aboriginal guide, shifted weight shyly from one foot to another as he talked to himself, wearing his whiteman's language about as easily as he wore his whiteman's clothes.

He stayed out while we went inside the incongruous modern-looking church.

I walked forward to look at the hand-carved mulga baptismal font and then, turning to look back at the pews, I saw, high on the back wall, the whitest Christ crucified you could imagine. Not even a decent touch of Middle East olive.

* * *

Out further on the banks of the Finke, we had a barbecue alongside the European house that Albert Namatjira built, neglected these days and rarely on the official tourist route. With some relish, Geoff told us that fullblooded Percy had been a meticulous caretaker until a jealous tribesman had put battery acid in his wine flagon and he "expired". Now the Aborigines think the site is haunted. They leave it to the goannas and the desert wind.

* * *

Back in the motel room, I'd graduated to Margaret Drabble and *The Millstone*. Rosamund recalls her sister's troubles in keeping her children "decent". Nicholas and Alexandra were not allowed to play with a particularly poor kid with a square, unexpressive face.

"Why ever not?" I asked, and there was doubtless a note of accusation in my voice, for Beatrice replied crossly, "Oh, it's all very well, but it really is quite impossible. I let them play at first but it was just out of the question, you've no idea of the things they got up to."

"No you're right, I haven't", I said, even more curious. "Do tell me."

"Well", she said, "I suppose I don't really mind accents and things, at least in theory, though that child is quite incomprehensible, she speaks in such an extraordinary fashion, but it's all the other things really that I just can't stand."

"Such as what?" I said.

"Oh, things like playing in the outside lavatory. I could never get them out of it. I was having to chase them out all the time. What they used to get up to in there, God alone knows, I don't like to think. And then she taught them such frightful words; they had one wonderful game which consisted of swinging on the garden gate and yelling Silly Bugger at every one that went by."

I laughed and so did Beatrice, but then she went on, "It's all very well, but people don't like it, and then they teach it to other children, and so on, and in the end our kids won't have anyone left to play with but her, because other parents won't put up with it even if I do, and I can hardly have mine ostracized for the sake of that, can I?"

* * *

"It's not the colour. It's just that they smell so", said the ancient English lady in the six seater 'plane as we sped towards Ayers Rock.

Sitting behind the pilot, I almost went crazy trying to crack the radio code. It seemed that Charlie and Romeo had something going for each other.

* * *

On the top of "the pebble" I wrote a forgettable poem in the "I-climbed-the-rock" book. Something about earth hath not anything to show more fair and ice cold beer.

* * *

We stopped at Ebenezer's Log Cabin coming back by road from Ayers Rock.

A naked Aboriginal male painted in discreet silhouette on a wall put me onto the urinal.

The cabin was a beautiful oasis. Immaculate lawns and juicy shrubbery, clipped to a nicety, surrounded the whiteman's fortress. I had myself a cold beer.

Across the road in the dust, we bartered for genuine artefacts made by the happy looking band of Aborigines camped there.

The kids, at home in the dust, eyed me shyly and then went on with their games.

Driving away from Ebenezer's, I could see the lone and level sands stretching far away.

* * *

Relaxed at nine thousand metres, heading for Adelaide, I wondered why I cheered when Alistair Maclean's irreverent hero, Cavell, lone operator, nobody's man, socked it verbally to the bureaucrats:

"I crossed to my desk, put the gun away and brought out the flask, money and slip of paper with the Warsaw address. I could feel the tightness in my face but I kept my voice quiet.

"Take your damned props, Martin and get out. You, too, Hardanger. I don't know what this stupid charade, this farrago of rubbish, was for and I'll be damned if you can make me care. Out! I don't like smart alecs making a fool out of me and I won't play mouse to any man's cat, not even the Special Branch's."

"Easy up now, Cavell," Hardanger protested. "I told you it was necessary and —."

"Let me talk to him", the man in khaki interrupted. He came round Hardanger and I could see him clearly for the first time. Army Officer, and no subaltern either, slight, spare, authoritative, the type I'm allergic to. "My name is Cliveden, Cavell. Major-General Cliveden. I must . . ."

"I was cashiered from the army for taking a swing at a Major-General", I interrupted. "Think I'd hesitate to do it now I'm a civilian? You, too. Out. Now!"

Suddenly, I flashed back to Matthew at the Mission, shifting from one foot to the other, hand shyly extended for his 50 cent pay off.

* * *

Full-circle, I found myself reconsidering Halliday and his sociolinguistic interface, Geoff and his dymo tape magic, Matthew and his secondhand language, childhood games in the outside lavatory, codes and signs designed to separate, and Ebenezer's Whiteman's Castle.

I still wonder about the ghosts of the natives around the cold waters of Ellery Gorge. I wonder, too, what secrets there are behind the door of the front bar of the Alice Springs Hotel.

I think I'm a little wiser about the sociolinguistic interface.

19 Do teachers really know what they are asking?

Take up Your Pens

Can you remember your school days? Can you remember warm, sleepy afternoons, the after-lunch lethargy which reduced you to watching the tree outside the window? Can you close your eyes and recall the hazy background and the droning voice of the teacher? Were you ever interrupted with a jolt, jarred back to reality by that emergency sixth sense which signalled that the time for reverie was over and that there was danger present? Did you ever return to the classroom just in time to hear those torturous words . . .

"Now I want you to take up your pens . . ."

Do you remember? The peace of the afternoon was shattered, the day was ruined. Your world was invaded and the panic started. You had to cut off all those thoughts which you had wandering around outside the classroom, and force yourself to concentrate on that blank sheet of paper which was in front of you. You probably did not even realize that for the past twenty minutes the teacher had been performing to a well established pattern, motivating you towards "good writing". All you knew when alerted to the task was the frustration of trying to write something—for the teacher.

Unfortunately, there are too many of us as teachers who are unable to recall our school memories. We quickly forget the view from the other side of the fence. We also teach a number of students whose school writing experiences were never ours.

As teachers, we have experienced some success at school writing. One has to "pass" writing in order to pass anything else to qualify as a teacher. Teachers have been able to perform adequately at writing tasks when they have been required. Writing is something they *can do*, no matter how painful it may be. Although there may be some teachers who have tasted writing failure (in a specific subject, or at a certain time) they have never been overwhelmed by it. Otherwise they wouldn't be teachers!

Think what it would be like to have suffered the school experience of writing failure! If it were not just discomfort or frustration that you felt, when asked to write, but futility and humiliation. Can you know what it is like to be tried every day and found wanting? Can you know what it is like to be tortured by picking up a pen?

There are kids to whom such an ordeal is all too familiar. Because teachers are a privileged group who have succeeded in school, it is unlikely that they have felt as these kids do. Not because they couldn't; rather because they are unaware. The school careers of teachers preclude such experiences. If teachers were aware of what they were really asking these kids, then perhaps they would ask different things.

Putting Teachers to the Test

With this idea in mind, I decided to simulate a context for teachers, in which writing posed a similar threat as it does to some of their students. I wanted to see if they could find out how it felt. And it wasn't going to be easy, because they were writing "successes" to start with.

My first attempt at being nasty was at a workshop at an English teachers' conference. I had been listening to a group of teachers complaining about the poor quality of the writing among today's students. There was consternation and concern. I didn't think it would be terribly fruitful if I simply asked why they thought students had difficulty in writing. Practical demonstrations were more in order.

This is how I started.

> "It worries me that you should find that the writing which the kids do is so awful. I get quite upset that our standards are dropping. It won't be long before no-one can write. I think we should do something, and quickly. And I think I have some of the answers.
>
> "It seems to me that one of the reasons students can't write, is that teachers can't write. I'm really appalled at the way some teachers write. I don't see how they can teach kids to write if they can't write themselves."

There was a reaction to this statement. Immediately the atmosphere within the room changed. Each teacher began to feel uneasy. It saddened me to see teachers so ready to devalue themselves, but if I wanted them to know what it was like to be a devalued kid, in a school, I had to persevere.

I proceeded to divide the class into groups, and told them I would be giving them a writing task to complete. The first group (and there was no random selection involved) consisted of all the males present. I did my utmost to appear intimidating to them.

112   THE SPITTING IMAGE

"I'm very interested in the standard of writing of teachers. I'd like to see how well you can write. I'm a lecturer at the university and I'm particular about 'good writing'. It is alarming that some teachers, particularly English teachers, write so dreadfully."

I continued along these lines, making mention of evaluation, the necessity for correctness, the desirability of extensive vocabulary and the suggestion that superior officers would be interested in knowing my assessment of their writing. I then gave this group one half hour to write a report on the conference. I left them, each showing signs of tension, furrowed brows and shifting feet; all with pens either poised or in mouth. No-one immediately commenced writing.

The second group was given the benefit of the "soft sell". I reduced the tension level and suggested that they might like to write to a friend about the day's happenings. They smiled back expressing relief and turned to their letter writing.

That there was really no need for them to write anything, was the way I prefaced my comments to the third group. I simply chatted with them for a few minutes. Then, almost as an afterthought I casually suggested that they might just like to jot something down for themselves, as everyone else was so occupied. A few of them began making "notes" (one started on a shopping list) and I deliberately ignored everyone until the half hour was up.

It was a warm, quiet and lazy afternoon, and group three, showing some signs of restlessness after about ten minutes, began to become engrossed in whatever it was that they were writing. At the end of the half hour, I was unethical and collected everything that everyone had written.

What are your predictions?

Group 1

From the group of threatened males, there was a little pile of writing which displayed all the signs of those writing under stress. Every piece was very short, punctuated by cross outs and alterations. Sentences had been begun and then abandoned. The writing was awkward, stilted and difficult to read. Their tension which I had witnessed when they had begun to write was transmitted through their writing. In their own words, they said it was *awful*.

There are a few samples, shown to advantage without the errors, alterations, and hesitation phenomena.

> "The main reason for my attendance at this conference is that because I feel it is necessary to participate in in-service courses, in order to help keep abreast with modern ideas. One is usually able to glean some valuable information from the variety of speakers who are assembled here for the occasion. It must be of assistance to those teachers in the field to be able to come and converse with experts in the area, about the more recent discoveries which are being made. They would return from the conference in a much more knowledgeable state, having profited from the opportunity to have access to those new ideas which they would otherwise not have come into contact with."

What has he told us? That there are speakers at the conference and new ideas? How much is there of value in this statement? How far does he share his ideas and thoughts? How far is the writer removed from his writing?

> "This conference has been exceedingly well organized and considerable effort has obviously been directed towards its arrangement. The executive is to be congratulated on its management of the proceedings. It has been planned with the conception of individual differences in mind, as there are many offerings which one may choose from. The necessary co-ordination involved to allow individuals their own peculiar combination of workshop topics is an improved innovation and a great deal of effort has been devoted to arranging it so that it is possible. The administration is very effective and there should be a vote of confidence put to the executive."

"One attends conferences out of an earnest desire to become more knowledgeable in one's subject area. This conference has fulfilled those expectations which I had formulated for it and I am convinced that it will provide me with a sound base for future reference in forthcoming times when a more theoretical framework is needed to act as reinforcement for my discussions with other teachers who seek my advice for application in the practical area of the classroom. I feel quite refreshed by all these new ideas."

The above three samples of writing indicate that the authors are quite familiar with the mechanics of writing—they can write. Perhaps it is that something interferes with the process when they come to write under certain conditions.

They had written in order to be judged from their writing. They produced something which belied their ability to write. No-one should be asked to make themselves as vulnerable as this group—not even kids!

Group 2

I was slightly disappointed with the second group, the letter writers. I thought their writing would have been better. It occurred to me that I had probably been too heavy handed with my opening remarks and that they were unable to escape from the idea that I, the teacher-as-examiner was the real audience. If they were writing to friends, they could not have been very good friends. There was an absence of warmth, a preoccupation with form, which is not usually characteristic of letter writing to peers.

These two samples speak for themselves.

"Dear . . .

I am at a conference in _____ and have so far found it quite interesting. It is always an advantage to mix with other teachers and 'talk shop'. I'm quite pleased that I have come to this one, although two hours at lunchtime seems to drag. It could be shorter I think. So far we have heard some interesting addresses and I am quite eager to return to the classroom and try out some of the new ideas that I have heard exchanged here . . ."

Again, this language is not so different from that of the first group. There is not the same awkwardness and convoluted style, but there is still evidence of self-consciousness in both the sentence structure and the choice of words. This is no free flowing letter to a friend. The next sample is a contrived attempt to develop the "familiar" style which is generally associated with letter writing.

"Dear . . .

I'm sure you'll excuse the delay since last I wrote but the pressures of work have been severe enough to allow me insufficient free time to indulge in the luxury of personal correspondence. I find this moment a rare pearl in that I have been requested to write this letter as part of an assignment at a conference which I am attending, and I see it as a golden opportunity to catch up on all the news."

The letter continues, but I see little need to quote it in full. The best thing to do with it would be to ask you how you would react if you received such a letter from a friend?

Group 3

The third group was beautiful! Because of the way in which I had structured the situation, I quickly glanced at the writing samples, before exposing them to public scrutiny. (I did not mention authors during the whole session; only the individual who had written the piece of writing was aware of its origin). One sample, which I will not include here for obvious reasons, was about a "bitch" at English conferences. It was one of the most refreshing pieces of writing I have ever read; it reflected the author's compelling need to write it. To sum it up, it was delicious.

Two samples were sufficiently personal that I simply put them aside after going no further than the first two lines. They were not meant for anyone else's eyes. But there are three samples which I feel I can include here without violating the privacy of the individuals who were involved.

This is writing which is really written "close to the self". It is not self conscious and awkward, not under threat of evaluation or assessment. There is no fear of punishment in this writing, but rather an ease with words. Would you like to see your students write like this?

> Conglomeration of teachers
> Conferences
> Smell the chalk — and talk and talk —
> They even look like
> Teachers
> And I wish
> I was outside
> Out of it all
> Where it is quiet and tranquil
> Not this bloody hassle
> Of pretentiousness and performance.
> Why the hell didn't I go to the beach?

Maybe if I hadn't screamed, sounded off again, what's the point, doesn't matter, wouldn't change, no reasons, just keep getting so angry, can't manage, no control, screams and storms—just want a quiet warm bed and go to sleep, electric blanket style-cocoon, *no*, too much, backwards and forwards, yo-yo, always back for more, masochistic? pointless, fruitless, hopeless, less, less—guts, more and more, where? don't just happen, work, effort, achieve, good middle class words, work to find guts, guts, blood and guts, gutsy, pulp and mess.

If only I could find the words, and I have always thought I had all the words—alright, never lost for words, arguing, debating, public speaking, essays, stories, always knew the words. But they are all formal occasions—when I need them the private times, away from all those other ears, I can't find them, I don't even know if I ever had them. Searching for a word—a clear word, a shorthand word—love won't do—debased and devalued. It's just not good enough. Need my own new vocabulary. Make them up? Be creative! Go forth and find the word! I know that's the answer—the question is *how*?

Je t'adore—hardly (that's the thou holier than me bit, the "worship" bit—that's not clean). Where do you get them from. They've all been messed up. Word association test—cheapened—adore, love, relationship? It's all so clumsy. Need something cool, caressing and committed, to touch and glow—even that, look at it. The ad men got it for Max Factor. They all have the tainted touch. It's the media. It leaves me nothing fresh. I don't even know where to start. The consumer culture, I've always been given my words. Now, when I want my own meanings, my own words, ones that aren't tarnished, I haven't got them. Teaching English? I'm a hypocrite. If I haven't got my own words of love, how can I teach anything that is worthwhile.

There is life in this writing. The authors have had something to say. Left alone, they have found their own areas to write about. And what they have said was valuable to all those teachers who were present at the workshop. The writing *spoke for itself*. There was no need for me to say anything.

Suddenly the teachers all looked at the writing that was there. They realized that if you are going to write for a "mark", something happens to the writing. Something goes wrong.

Why do Students Write Badly?

I still do not know whether I adequately answered the question—why do students write badly?—maybe I just asked a different one. But there were quizzical looks on the faces of those around, and a buzz which gave way to a clamour about assessment, evaluation and marking.

It's not difficult to make a situation so threatening that people are paralysed when it comes to writing. All you have to do is to make them vulnerable, self conscious, unsure of themselves. All you have to do is ask them to be judged according to the words, and immediately they start to have difficulty finding the right words.

These teachers had had difficulty finding the right words. They were the "experts" with writing in the school, but place them in the same situation as their students and teachers will tie themselves in exactly the same sort of knots.

Tell teachers they are going to be judged when they put pen to paper, remind them of the composition correction code, emphasize that their future depends on the quality of their writing and, not surprisingly, teachers will write very badly.

And it would be so easy to declare smugly that the reason students cannot write is because teachers cannot write. Which would just go to prove that it is always possible to go round in educationally ever diminishing circles until there is absolutely nowhere to turn. Unless you are prepared to ask whether teachers really know what they are asking when they give the command for pupils to pick up their pens and perform.

Because if they did know what they were asking, they would find a more reasonable and valid way for allowing writing to emerge. They would be intent on removing the obstacles, instead of making more.

20 Scratch an education expert . . .

Who are the Experts?

When the Railways department has trouble with a bridge, it quite frequently goes to the expert and consults the Professor of Engineering.

When fishermen find that there is something wrong with the fish, they will seek the assistance of the expert and ask the marine biologist at the university for an explanation.

When a medico is unable to make decisions about a complicated pregnancy, he may seek the advice of the academic who has more expertise than he and refer the patient to the Professor of Obstetrics for a diagnosis.

Even the Treasury and the Reserve Bank seek the assistance of the academic experts when faced with a financial problem.

Where do the teachers go? Who are the experts in education? Who are the ones with more expertise than the teachers? To what wiser, more informed, more experienced authority can teachers appeal when they are confronted with problems? If teachers feel that they do not have sufficient information at their disposal to make a decision, where do they turn for advice?

How far would teachers get if they took their problems to the education experts within the university? The question is purely rhetorical. There can be no definite answer because teachers just don't do it. I have never known a teacher to refer any problem to a university education department. I have never known an academic educationist to be called in to a school for the benefit of his wisdom.

On the contrary, whenever I have asked teachers why they don't take the problem to the education experts, I have been viewed askance, treated as a fool and subjected to the following rationale:

"You would have to be joking!"

How many education experts can you name who know anything significant about schools? It's years since many of them have been in them or near them. They just don't know what they're talking about when it comes to teaching. They couldn't survive a day in the classroom. They live in a dream world which has nothing to do with schools. We don't even speak the same language!

Being cast in this less than flattering light, I began to ask questions and to make comparisons. It does seem to be true that there is little love lost between the teachers and the education experts. There is not even any evidence that there is much communication between these two closely related groups. And there is a great deal of mutual contempt.

The education experts displayed their contempt for teachers when they commented that if they thought teachers could understand what they were saying, then they would stop saying it, because it must be neither clever nor complex. And teachers displayed their contempt for education experts by declaring them vacant. This can hardly be described as a desirable educational climate.

Desensitizing the Experts

I began to ask whether this mutual disregard appeared anywhere outside education. Were there any other professions where the experts were held in such low regard and where those out in the field were treated with such scorn? Do architects speak so scathingly of the architectural academics? Do the academics show such disdain towards the practising architects? Are there the same divisions between solicitors and legal academics?

And the answer is no. I had to come to the conclusion that the education experts have been desensitized. When I suggested to some academic engineers that perhaps they were not equipping their students with the means of being engineers they were horrified. When I suggested the same to the medical academics, there was almost a panic. But when I made the same criticism to the education academics they smiled knowingly and reassured me patronisingly that this was understandable. I mean no one knows what makes a good teacher. Thank goodness someone knows what makes a good doctor.

But the tolerant attitude of the education experts was not always obvious. There were other areas where they were quite emphatic.

Knowing What's Good for You

When the students (some of whom are already teachers) began to insist that the education experts were not providing the courses which they wanted, that the courses were not even vaguely connected to teaching, and the students began to document what they did want and did need, and why, it was quite difficult to find a receptive education expert. They were quite secure in their knowledge and very positive about their ability to make pronouncements on what was the necessary diet for a good teacher. They could comfortably rationalize that the students were not in a position to know what was good for them. They were adamant that such a decision must be left to the experts.

It seemed a strange compromise. On the one hand the education experts graciously admitted that there was no research available to substantiate that courses in educational philosophy and the history of the Board of Secondary Education necessarily equipped teachers for the task of teaching. But on the other, they were prepared to conclude that if teachers were unable to perceive the value of such courses, then this was the fault of the teachers. The teachers obviously did not know what was good for them.

It was alright for the experts to say that it was impossible to verify the link between theories on the nature of teaching, and the actual task of teaching. But when the teachers said it, it just proved how little they knew and understood.

And so the experts persisted in giving courses on the structure of knowledge, and the more the students objected the more the education experts were confirmed in their belief that teachers were not very bright people. And the more such courses were inflicted on the students, the more they became convinced that the education experts knew nothing about teaching.

While the education experts give out their expertise, the learners (students and teachers) part company with them. Each group goes its own merry way. The experts become more sophisticatedly expert and the teachers become more belligerently antagonistic. And never the twain shall meet. . . .

The Humble Teacher

The architect does not seem to suffer from the law of diminishing returns when he becomes a "theoretical academic". There seems to be room to accommodate the theoretical economist. The expertise of the legal academic is not dismissed on the grounds that it has nothing to do with law.

What has gone wrong for the education expert? The answer is simple. If engineers have to demonstrate their expertise by building bridges, and mathematicians have to be able to demonstrate their expertise by solving mathematical problems, then education experts have to be able to demonstrate their expertise by being able to teach. They don't do that, nor do they want to. Teaching has a very low priority with education experts.

There is something unique about the education lecturer, because before he attained such elevated heights, *he was a humble teacher*. And most of them would prefer to forget that! The economics lecturer was an economist; the biology lecturer a biologist; but the education lecturer was a teacher. And this may produce some very strange behaviour patterns.

Because first of all teaching does not rate very highly in our community, nor does it enjoy the same prestige as medicine or law; it is a poor relation. Perhaps our education experts are apologetic about their origins. They may wish to remove themselves completely from any incriminating links with their previously impoverished background. They might find it essential to disown those who knew them in less attractive circumstances. They may have to divorce themselves from the embarrassment that goes with teaching.

> *If status is measured by the distance they have progressed from the school, then it is in the interest of the education expert's prestige to make that distance as great as possible!*

Medicos have no such vested interest in escaping their medical backgrounds when they become medical academics; legal academics need not separate themselves from their previous profession, but there seems to be a lot of evidence that the educational academics need to divest themselves of anything which may remotely connect them with teaching.

Widening the Gap

There are many ways they can make a significant contribution to widening the gap between teacher training institutions and teachers. They can become superior and arrogant. This is almost guaranteed to make teachers feel inadequate and uncomfortable. It will serve very well to remind them that they are in the presence of one who is much better endowed (because he/she has the ability to "get out of teaching") and the students will be suitably impressed. They can smile disdainfully when anything "practical" is mentioned until the students feel too awkward to ask anything about teaching.

They can deliberately not publish any of their opinions or "research" in teachers' journals because it would only "lower" their academic reputation. They can take great pride in their ability to be unable to communicate with teachers.

They can adopt a refined stance and indicate that they have no wish to be contaminated by the vulgarities of teaching; they can subtly convey the impression that if any of their students were worth their salt they would demonstrate it by getting out of teaching. That is why "bright" education students are discouraged from becoming teachers. That is why education experts treat those students who aspire to be good teachers as failures.

But sometimes (as is to be expected) teachers are quite dense. They are very slow to get this message that the academic educationist is a superior being. This calls for more blatant and direct action on the part of the expert. This is where language can be a convenient weapon.

They can make sure that the teachers cannot possibly understand what they are saying. They can mystify them with their language. This is a very effective way of reinforcing their advanced status. They can cleverly disguise the most basic and rudimentary elements of common sense under such erudition and sophistication that they are no longer recognizable. Education experts could never be criticised for the efficient way in which they perform their window dressing task. That's why they call lessons "instructional episodes". By the time you have deciphered what they mean you are lost, floundering in a sea of pretentious words and unable to find your way ashore.

"It is hardly surprising that relations between teacher training institutions and the schools have been strained; the 'higher' institutions wander into a limbo of intellectual self indulgence, and of snobbish scorn for those who continue to struggle in the schools; while the 'real' teachers grow more puzzled, irritated or amused by the latest fashions in educational theory that the student teachers bear, unsuspecting and innocent into the schools during school practice."[1]

At the heart of every educational expert there is a denial of teaching. That is why they do not perceive the incongruity of lecturing on the inadequacies of lecturing as a teaching method. That is the explanation behind the tired old joke of being lectured to in the most boring and monotonous manner about the inadvisability of a monotonous speaking voice.

There is no way that education experts can practise what they preach. To do so would relegate them to the lowly depths of being a teacher. They must preserve the distance. Their justification rests on being able to prove that they are no longer teachers.

That is why they can dictatorially devise a course on the value of pupil participation in planning a curriculum. That is why they can stipulate rigid requirements for an assignment on creativity. That is why they can dogmatically deliver their views, for one full hour, without interruption, on learning as a two way process. That is why they can set an examination on the topic of the shortcomings of examinations as an educational practice. That is why teachers and students think that the education experts are absurd.

It is no wonder that people who are subjected to teacher training courses, conducted by individuals who wish to prove that they are no longer teachers, feel cheated. It is no wonder that they are constantly accusing their lecturers of hypocrisy. It's no wonder that they continually complain that the education degree has nothing to do with teaching. How else could you identify education experts? They wouldn't be experts if they were associated with teaching!

Educationists are experts at keeping an audience at bay; they are experts in displaying expertise; they are at home with pretentiousness. They can use language to intimidate and to remind students that they are a long, long way behind, while aspiring to being a teacher. They can parade their knowledge under cover of such confusing jargon, that even if what they are saying is remotely relevant to teachers, there is no way they will guess. They are committed to an impenetrable barrier. It has been known for a long time that education experts are not saying much which is of any value for teachers. But that it might be a survival tactic is perhaps not as readily recognized. The real crux of the problem is to determine whether it is necessary. Could it be that, when deprived of all their elaborate ruses, there is nothing there to say? While teacher training institutions maintain their present priorities, education experts will have to maintain their absurd practices. There is no other way for them to go.

Change?

It is almost too much to envisage any change. Can you imagine what it would be like if education experts were to practise what they preach? How on earth could they cope with deschooling? If education experts were to be committed to teaching, the ramifications would be felt throughout the entire system.

They would have to start "interacting" with people; they would have to listen to the students; they would have to see each individual in terms of worth and value; *they would have to find some contribution to make.*

They would have to face the fact that it is possible to be a good teacher, with or without the present teacher training, and conversely, that it is possible to be a bad teacher with or without the training. They would have to look at engineers and chemists with respect. Because it's not possible to be a good engineer or a good chemist without training. They would have to admit that they didn't know the answers and be prepared to start learning. And they would have to start learning about themselves!

Can they face the fact that it is people who count; that it is the *personal* qualities which are important, or are they too frightened by the prospect of their own failure? Could they possibly provide education students with rich and varied experiences in order to stimulate their growth towards being rich and varied personalities? Could educational experts really tolerate individual differences? Could they give verification to the value of concepts such as open mindedness, diversity and change? Could they give substance to the value of human dignity?

At the moment, someone would have to teach the education experts before they could reasonably be expected to teach others. That's why teachers don't take their problems to the education experts!

Notes

1. Summerfield, Geoffrey and Tunnicliffe, Stephen (ed). *English in Practice.* Cambridge University Press. 1971, p. 3.

21 Who's afraid of the illiteracy scare? A personal view

It is interesting to note that the recently tabled Bullock Report on English teaching in the U.K. takes a moderate, non-alarmist line on the matter of literacy while acknowledging a need for improvement. I have yet to be convinced that literacy is at an alarmingly low level in our schools. To me, the evidence presented by many of the scaremongers often seems tantamount to saying that 50 per cent of the children are below average. And "literacy" itself is a word for all seasons, sometimes covering the ability to put full stops and commas in the right place, sometimes referring to fundamental skills in reading and sometimes referring to "culture", to awareness and appreciation of the literary heritage.

Teachers are no different from other human beings in their tendency to whitewash the past and to disparage the here and now. Last year's classes are invariably seen as superior to the latest crop of numbskulls. Scapegoats are easy to find: the "idiot" box; inane advertising; teaching the whole word method; new English curricula that don't demand Shakespeare; and the passing of external examinations. So from early secondary school through to the halls of the universities the cries go up that "kids today don't read or can't read", that "they can't write essays", that "it's about time we got back to some good old-fashioned grammar".

How is it, then, that borrowings from libraries by children have never been higher; that educational testing experts in New South Wales had to raise the difficulty of test items in certain forms of traditional language testing so that they could properly challenge the clientele; that the level of complexity and intricacy of subject matter in upper secondary schools seems to get higher every year; that more and more children are reaching higher and higher levels of education? Where precisely is the decline and what are the symptoms?

I think it would be interesting to test whether or not students today are expected to grasp more difficult concepts than say comparable students of twenty years ago. I think it would be relatively easy to prove at least that schools expect a far wider spectrum of language skills from students today—including the ability to speak independently and spontaneously in the classroom.

It is quite likely that a comparison of 1955 and 1975 would show that while the language expectations of the school have risen, those of society at large have decreased. Newspapers, particularly the popular brands, are probably getting easier to read every year and visual and oral means of communication are continuing apace to displace the written word.

Unfortunately there seems to be very little research which might show that children today are at least no worse than their mothers and fathers, linguistically speaking. Rather we hear the recurring snipers, the pedants and nit pickers who are always ready to forsake the essence and fasten onto the paraphernalia of language, the outer dressings of spelling, punctuation and "received" pronunciation, of split infinitives and ultimate prepositions. The essence of language is meaning making and meaning taking, the skill or art of understanding and being understood.

Any attack on allegedly falling standards of literacy is of dubious value unless it defines what it means by literacy and can give clear evidence of decline. Nor is it fair to make blanket comparisons since more and more children are staying on longer at secondary school. To uphold say average Grade 12 achievement in 1965 against that in 1975 is a false comparison even if proper retrospective measurement could be devised. I think that, given the difficulty of measuring past achievement by past generations, we should abandon emotive and subjective tirades about decline in literacy and concentrate instead on what *is* and what *is desirable*.

What we need is across the board co-operation by all concerned. If a teacher or university lecturer or parent, for that matter, complains about the poor language performance of students or of a particular child, with the implication that something should be done about it, I am tempted to ask, "What are you doing, or prepared to do, about it?" This is not to deny that there may be a real problem but it seems to me that the "something — should — be — done — about — it" complaint, especially if it comes from prestigious university sources, too often leads to the game of "remediation buckpassing" now becoming so fashionable in our schools.

After the finger pointing and scapegoat hunting has found some suitable sacrifice to offer up to the complainant and to the media, administrators often make administrative gestures.

And so we find university English departments pressured to run courses in how to write, or secondary schools establishing reading clinics or infant schools re-introducing phonetics. Good for appeasing administrative consciences but are they really solving the problems?

Before we race off in all directions at once, we should surely ask, "Give us your proofs." But perhaps while we wait for proofs, we could be getting on with some sensible low key measures to get to the root causes of illiteracy.

As I have said above, "literacy" and "illiteracy" are much mangled concepts. For the purposes of the following short discussion I shall define literacy as the ability to receive and understand meanings and to convey meanings couched in the written words according to the demands of particular situations occurring in an individual's life. In other words, if a second year university student is unable to decode his geology text book then he might be said to be illiterate with respect to geology *at that level*. This, then, is a very broad definition and a very generous concession to those who want to argue that there is widespread illiteracy in our educational institutions.

On the other hand, it may lead to an indictment of geology lecturers and geology text writers rather than of the English teachers who have taught that student over the years. It is not unlikely that that same student could breeze through Tolstoy's *War and Peace* and write admirably cogent love letters to his sweetheart.

From what we know from researchers about reading and writing, we can say with some confidence that reading and writing are not unitary achievements. When you have learnt to swim, you have learnt to swim, but writing, for instance, is quite different. One can be quite safe and functional in one situation and completely out of one's depth in another. The writing task is affected by the audience, by the nature of the assignment, by the subject matter, by the availability to the writer of appropriate language resources, by past experience in similar situations and by the purpose (or motivation). So, perhaps when the professor of geology complains about student illiteracy he should be qualifying his statements to say that the students cannot write geology reports and, having acknowledged that, he might then be led to the realization that the students had never been taught the ground rules of writing geology reports.

Furthermore, if writing is essentially the art of marshalling language to make meanings, then it could well be that the reason for the so-called illiteracy is not the inability to marshal language but a more deep-seated lack of meaning to be conveyed. That is, the teaching of geology may have been so obscure or so poorly assimilated by the student that he fails to understand key concepts. Those teachers who have marked innumerable essays do not need the experts to tell them that a breakdown in syntax is more than likely a symptom of confused thinking.

The torturing of the written word, disjunctions, redundancies and so on, often disappear when the writer embarks on a subject where he is at ease with his audience and in command of his thoughts. Stiltedness, artificiality and nonsensical juxtapositions may be the result of pathetic attempts to ape the style of learned geology textbooks, attempts where the focus is on "going through the motions" rather than on making personal knowledge communicable. Such students put together strips of other people's words indiscriminately to signify nothing. Sadly, it seems, they have perceived the assignment as a language game called "try to camouflage what you don't know in order to impress the teacher".

This small illustration at the university level leads me to make a point which, I suggest, applies at all levels of education, namely that alleged illiteracy should always be examined in the context of the *total language* situation in which it is evidenced. Failure to treat the act of communication as an intricately complex phenomenon could lead to ineffectual remediation aimed at one symptom while the cause still prevails.

With respect, I am therefore led to question the present outlay in Australia of vast amounts of money on reading laboratories and specialist developmental reading teachers and reading equipment while basically the total language environment of our schools remains unchanged. At best I suspect that this is temporary "patching up" activity; at worst it could lead to the trivialization of communication removed from the real world to the sterility of the clinic.

If teachers are to diagnose the causes of illiteracy in depth and are then to take effective steps to overcome perceived problems, they should not hedge from the possibly embarrassing task of looking at their own language behaviour in schools as a contributing factor. For instance, if the tone of the teacher is constantly formal and impersonal and if he constitutes the sole audience for most of the students' writing, then it may well be that the student will tend to "freeze up" or to experience such difficulty in relating to his audience that his writing will appear crippled and incoherent.

Allied to such problems is what could be called the political dimension of illiteracy. How many children in our schools do not learn to read and write either because they do not choose to play the language games of the middle classes or because they are so threatened by the strangeness of the school culture that they withdraw knowing intuitively that silence is the best safeguard against censure and discrimination?

From the moment a working class child sets foot in school he or she is likely to be affected by many values which are alien, values transmitted through beginning readers, teachers' injunctions and the often unspoken but pervasive, unquestioned assumption that reading and writing are good and necessary skills. There is a resulting tug on the child to put aside, at least in school, many of the habits and behaviours of home and the neighbourhood. Even in the most sympathetic of schools, failure to read, and later to write, is usually attended by an anxiety which is likely to compound.

Against all the evidence of many "illiterates" who live quite happily and successfully, educationists generally persist in talking of literacy as a survival skill when, in truth, it is a social selection skill. There are social penalties, status penalties and employment penalties, that is money penalties, for reading and writing failures.

For those who learn to read and to write uncritically at a minimal, functional level the rewards are those of belonging and the comfort of conformity. Such literacy means that the ruling classes and the mind benders can more easily exercise social control over the bulk of the populace who are complacent in the knowledge that they can read and write enough to get by and comfortable because they are largely unaware that they are being manipulated—just literate enough to receive the message.

The illiterates who survive, and they all do, are a threat to order. Relying on the spoken word, they make their way in the world never having received "the truth" as represented in school textbooks and newspapers. Admittedly television will do some of the work of representing "reality" according to the power classes but these illiterates are likely to be cussedly independent, non-conforming, perhaps even downright rebellious because they have not been washed over with the written word.

In my view, rebellious illiteracy is preferable to the literacy of no man's land, "passive literacy", the educational equivalent of that pretty purple weed, Paterson's curse, or "salvation Jane" as we call it in South Australia. I say this in the belief that the major goal of education is to lead children to think critically and to make new meanings. Which reminds us of the geology student pasting together someone else's words, unable to assimilate and transform "external" knowledge and make it his own. I have suggested that the geology fraternity itself might take some blame for this "passive literacy" but I think that the cause might lie more generally in a succession of school environments including the university where the emphasis has been on receiving knowledge rather than on learning to think, writing to think, and reading to think. It stands to reason that if your own meanings are constantly undervalued or ignored you will soon learn to appropriate the legitimized meanings of an authority in order to feel "a piece of the continent". For such self-sacrifice, authority may even put the seal on your education by conferring a certificate of graduation. And the working class child who graduates receives a bonus—the promise of social mobility.

Is this a too cynical view of schools and schooling? What *do* we know about total school language environments?

Research conducted by a project team from the University of London Institute of Education into the development of writing abilities, where writing in all subjects from 11-18 year olds was sampled, revealed that of the order of *80 per cent* of the writing in history, science and geography was to convey information, and that in 61 per cent of the cases in geography, 69 per cent in history and 87 per cent in science, the intended audience was the teacher in his role of examiner or assessor. Another way of putting this finding is to say that children in the secondary schools, at least in this sample, spend much of their energy trying to become more literate by conveying memorised facts to someone who already has the information (the teacher). This same research reveals that, except in English and religious education, students write almost exclusively in the transactional mode. Researchers found very little writing where the author was allowed the luxury of making personal remarks. Furthermore there was almost no writing where the writer was tentatively framing hypotheses, or speculating or wondering. What little personal or expressive writing there was, shrivelled away the higher up the secondary scale the child progressed.

On this evidence, the drive of the secondary school in the area of writing seems to be progressively towards a special but narrow band of the language spectrum which might be called "writing for examinations". Indeed, there is even some evidence to suggest that as students concentrate more on this kind of writing, the overall quality of their writing might be deteriorating. (Dr Harold Rosen's unpublished PhD thesis, University of London, suggests this.) Full-bodied literacy actively and critically engaged in real acts of communication may never be achieved as the potentially rich store of personal language is allowed to haemorrhage away at the end of the secondary school. I would guess that Australia is not likely to be much different from England in this regard.

An examination of the reading and writing behaviour of a matriculation candidate in Australia might well uncover large quantities of a sophisticated kind of meta-language, unlike any acts of communication in the world outside school. Would one find reading for pleasure? Or creative story writing? And what about audiences? Is there ever opportunity to explain some science or geography to someone who does not know? How much of the languaging would be revealed as rehearsal and dummy run as opposed to "the real thing"?

By continually resorting to these untried speculations, I am simply underlining the complexity of the literacy question and the almost complete lack of documentation of what is done in Australian schools. This complexity is surely no excuse for putting the central problems into the too hard basket and turning instead to half-hearted covering up and mending activity.

Let me summarize the above comments before suggesting a few simple new directions in the quest for full-bodied, active literacy.

- There is no proof that standards of so-called "literacy" are falling. No one would deny, however, that there are problems to be solved.
- The essence of literacy is the ability to receive and make meanings through and with the written word.

- There are no simple answers to perceived problems in the field of literacy. Thus, isolated remedial reading drives (for instance), are likely to be ineffectual.
- In searching for ways of improving literacy, the total language community of children must be explored.
- It may be that teachers who complain of the illiteracy of students in their subject area should look to their own teaching as a possible cause.
- Schools tend to be middle class language preserves and could therefore be at fault in setting up forbidding culture barriers which become literacy barriers for many working class and migrant children.
- Literacy is not a survival skill; it is a social selection skill.
- Functional literacy, "enough to get by on", might well be re-named "passive literacy" if it simply fits children to accept other people's meanings. "Active" literacy, on the other hand, is likely to be subversive of the status quo.
- Schools should be primarily engaged in promoting learning to think independently.
- There is evidence to suggest that a wide section of secondary schools may be progressively limiting the language options of the student. Answers tend to be valued more highly than speculation at all levels.

I should add that the power of literacy depends on the richness of the language resources brought to the literacy act and that these resources are largely built up through talk.

Given the above, I should like to see some of the following things happen in the service of literacy.

- Wide scale introduction of beginning reading materials which emphasise meaning and relate to the culture of the children learning to read.
- Less rush towards reading and writing in the infant school and more emphasis on "oracy" at all levels.
- Teacher education courses in the role of language in learning to be compulsory for all intending teachers at all levels and in all subject areas.
- Each school staff, across the curriculum, to formulate a school policy on the language environment of the school with a view to promoting learning in and through language.

- Each teacher to teach the language and special forms of his own subject area.
- Greater efforts to provide children in schools with a wide range of audiences and a wide range of language situations involving real operations with language as opposed to exercises.
- Less emphasis on the teacher as examiner and more options in all subjects for hypothesizing and open-ended speculation in talking and writing.
- A thorough-going investigation, and if necessary modification, of the language of textbooks with respect to two major criteria: clarity of communication to the intended audience and cultural balance.
- Multifaceted school-based teacher enquiries into the language environment of a particular school aimed at action to overcome problems.
- Documentation and investigation of the language of universities and tertiary institutions.
- An Australia-wide campaign to acquaint professional educators and laymen alike with what is presently known about language, including the irrefutable evidence that the teaching of English grammar (any grammar) is of no value in promoting active literacy.

Maybe some of the above strategies will take shape during the late seventies. Even so, it will become increasingly difficult to sell literacy to many children unless teachers can show that reading and writing are personally satisfying ways of reaching out to the world and of making new and exciting meanings. If it is seen as a dreary middle class hoop, who will blame them for not jumping?

22 *Please don't take this personally*

"Who's Afraid of the Illiteracy Scare" was an article commissioned by a certain editor of a certain journal. It was not acceptable to him in the form in which it appears in the previous chapter.

Although I have since revised the article myself, I include it in this book with all its original imperfections so that you can appreciate the humour and irony of the correspondence which it provoked between the editor and me.

A letter from the editor dated 14 March 1975 set my teeth on edge. As he has copyright on his own letters I am not able to give the actual text. What follows is, I think, an accurate summary of the contents, but I regret that I cannot re-create the flawless "officialese" of the correspondence.

I was conventionally his dear Mr. Boomer. He informed me that because of editorial policy he would like to see some minor changes in my article. In particular he felt it would be better if it were written in the third person in a more formal style.

He had directed his editorial staff to prepare an edited version and he would send me a draft for my approval and comment. A short bibliography would be appreciated. I was his sincerely.

I replied at once, with studied good humour:

"Dear . . . . . .,

I write in reply to your letter regarding the article 'Who's Afraid of the Illiteracy Scare?'

A close reading of the article should convince you that there is a reason of central importance for the style and tone in which it is presented. My medium is part of my message.

I am arguing that a root cause of illiteracy could be the denial of direct personal expression in our schools. Take it further and I might also argue that a root cause of the 'illiteracy' of teachers with regard to many educational articles could be the indirectness, impersonality and forced formality under which they so often labour.

You will understand, then, why I find your suggestions for 'defusing' my writing almost as insulting as your direction to the editorial staff to edit it, not because I resent criticism but because you display an insensitivity to my message.

Could it be that you and your staff have fallen into the old English teacher habit of responding more to the form of the writing than to the essence?

You imply politely but nevertheless with condescension that you find my writing unacceptable measured against the 'standards' of your editorial policy. My linguistic table manners don't quite suit your company.

Respond to my meanings. Tell me that you find something not clear, or contradictory or untrue. I welcome such response. But don't turn up your nose at good, strong, personal writing.

Of course, I could have written it in your 'style'. I have written that way before. As a graduate of a university English faculty, I can play that game well.

Before writing, I studied articles in your past journals, quite closely, and I deliberately chose to offer you something different perhaps as an indirect criticism.

Why do you find the first person an embarrassment? Is there something polluting about my attempt at some intimacy with my reader? Would it really be more objective if I said, 'Given the current state of research in this area, it would appear . . .', instead of, 'I think'?

Do you want to reduce your contributors' voices to a norm? Why not loosen your editorial stays a little? I'm sure that (you) would survive the publication of my largely unedited voice.

I don't mind if you attach an editorial comment saying you find my tone and style somewhat disturbing in one who purports to teach English.

Anyway, you can take it that I will not consent to the neuter sex change, nor to the embalming. Should you decide to let me have my way, I shall be pleased to supply a quite extensive bibliography, sub-headings, a photograph and details of my recent publications.

Since I am not hopeful that you will let me through unexpurgated, I shall wait on your reply before sending this information. Please do not dismiss me before considering closely what I offer.

Yours sincerely,
GARTH BOOMER."

I waited, as you may imagine, with some eagerness for the reply. Obviously, I had not made myself clear because on 4 April 1975 I received a meticulously re-written version of my article, third person and all, with a letter from the editor.

He informed me that the edited draft of my article which he had renamed *Who's Afraid of Literacy* was enclosed. He acknowledged that I had made some interesting points in my last letter but he also pointed out that as an editor he had responsibilities to publishers and readers.

In his opinion my article was too long and faulty in style. He felt my message should be concise and clear and he assured me that the edited version did not distort my style.

Indeed he had shown the edited version to various experts who confirmed this opinion. He urged me to consult other experts and to ring him if I was not satisfied.

He felt that it would be a pity if the article were not published. I was his sincerely.

I read the new version in a state of shock. I hardly recognized it. I might have been reading the work of a stranger. It was so convincing, so authoritative. I almost believed it. Pure third person perfect.

My 'phone conversation with the editor was absurd. He refused to become a person and I got angry. The intensity of my anger surprised me.

The next two letters crossed. Once more he ignored my anger (15 April 1975).

He could understand, thanks to my 'phone call, that I did not find all the changes acceptable and so he invited me to submit the article again including the changes I would countenance. However, he reminded me that it should be as short as possible. Once again, he assured me that he would be disappointed if the article were not published. I was his sincerely.

By now I had started to develop a sense of audience. My anger became tempered with devilment and I wrote (15 April 1975):

"Dear . . . . . .,

You and I are engaged in a little game which might be called 'say what you mean' or conversely 'mean what you say'. Either way I have to chuckle at your signing off 'yours sincerely'. Let me edit your letter (ever so slightly) to see if I can help you to imagine sitting in my shoes as I received your letter:

Dear Mr. Boomer,

I enclose a better version of your article 'Who's Afraid of the Illiteracy Scare?'

I received your letter of 17 March and note that you know nothing about journalism and editing and very little about writing educational articles. Your writing is long-winded and your message is not matched with your style.

Although I almost dared to agree with you on a couple of points, you can't expect me to print your work. Our readers don't want to be offended and they haven't got time to waste working out your meanings. We save them as far as possible from thinking. Could I also try to fob you off with the line that it takes a lot of money to include a few hundred more words?

My aim was to give a digest of your article and to make it sound acceptable. Several independent journalists and teachers whose names I won't give you, think that they perfectly understand your message and that I have done a brilliant job in re-capturing that very message. In fact, I'm very pleased with it myself.

Read what I have written; realize how wrong you are and how right I must be. If you don't believe me, have the sense to do exactly what I did and show it to an expert who agrees with me. I'll pay for the 'phone call so that you can apologise.

I'm really being so polite to you because it will be a nuisance if you withdraw consent at this stage.

See reason.

Yours condescendingly,
. . . ."

I have shown the above version to my wife who has written and read as many letters as any other normal person of her age and she thinks that I have done a fairly good job coming to grips with what you mean.

But I'm not at all satisfied that you have said what you mean. Therefore, I am going to sift through your edited version to see if I can find some clues as to what might really be offending you. . . .

I feel like an urchin who, entering a church, has asked the vicar to "pray for all us poor little bastards in the streets", only to be told "you mustn't talk like that in here my boy". Still, I'm a pretty sharp fellow and hope to learn how to use words proper from you.

Lesson one

Take "scare" out of the title. It is by definition the function of a scare to engender fear. Furthermore, "scare" used thus as a noun is not good educated usage. But worst of all the title is inflammatory, taking the view that there is an illiteracy scare in Australia and implying that some people have a vested interest in provoking fear. The simple solution is to eliminate that one multi-offensive word. Now look at the title. It has taken on a pleasing generality. It is no longer necessarily tied to the present educational scene. And yet it still retains the "grabby" directness of the original. Just a little unfortunate, that the built in allusion to the big bad wolf, and more indirectly to Virginia, is not now so clear.

Lesson two

"Scare mongers would have us believe . . ." instead of "I have yet to be convinced that" . . . "literacy is at an alarmingly low level in our schools".

Here we must first note a rule which will apply throughout . . . Get rid of "I" at all costs, even if it sometimes means telling half-truths. In fact, it is essential to get rid of this word so that people will swallow the idea. You get around this by pretending that lots of people say these things. In fact, if you're really clever you can make out that nobody said it.

Some examples:
- "I am led to question", . . . is easily transformed to, "(it) should not go unchallenged".
- "At best, I suspect that" becomes "Remedial reading can at best be . . ."
- "In my view rebellious illiteracy is preferable" becomes "Rebellious illiteracy seems preferable".

Very simple and very safe.

Lesson three

"How is it then, that borrowings from libraries by children have never been higher?" becomes "Borrowings by children from libraries have never been higher".

Here you will note economics — 14 words versus 9 — a nett saving of about 36% — and as a bonus you get rid of the argumentative tone conveyed by the question. You also help the busy reader who doesn't want to have to stop and ponder the question. This is what is called saving the reader from thinking.

Lesson four

Consider the edited sentence: "instead, we hear the voice of those who are always ready to forsake the essence of language for its paraphernalia".

We shan't linger on why "instead" is better than "rather" since everybody knows that "rather" cannot be used as a connective. Rather, we shall point to the crucial replacement of "snipers, pedants and nit pickers" with the "voice of those". ("Voice" not "voices".) One cannot allow a well known educational author to appear in public in the company of such words. For the sake of the teaching profession, it is the duty of editors to sober the poor fellow up, at least to give the appearance that he has a grip on himself.

But there is another reason. Perfectly decent citizens, with a perfectly normal concern about illiteracy, may mistakenly recognize themselves and take offence.

Lesson five

When editing your work, develop a nose for "semantic stench". This will enable you to weed out words like "the idiot box" and substitute "television". The former has all sorts of judgmental overtones, whereas "television" is suitably bland.

Take also the offensive reference to the middle classes in the following sentence:

How many children in our schools do not learn to read and write either because they do not choose to play the language games of the middle classes or because they are so threatened by the strangeness of the school culture that they withdraw knowing intuitively that silence is the best safeguard against censure and discrimination".

Deal with this by substituting "the language games of *an alien group*", thereby ensuring that the middle classes do not have to feel uncomfortable.

You should also outlaw "dummy run", "no man's land", "mangled", "race off" and references to "Paterson's Curse". These words have a tang, a raciness, out of place in a serious educational article.

Lesson six

Following on from lesson five, you should be most wary about retaining any attempts at humour. Educational articles are not funny.

So "racing off in all directions at once" and "Salvation Jane" go the way of all flesh.

"Bulldust!"

Lesson seven

If you are close to the seat of political power, you have to be polite.

Protect, but do it subtly. "Administrators make administrative gestures" is too direct (and what's more, it is redundant, isn't it?). It suggests that administrators might be to blame. It is less obvious if you say, "remedies often take the form of administrative gesture".

See if we can defuse the following:

"Such literacy means that the ruling classes and the mind benders can more easily exercise social control over the bulk of the populace."

This is a key sentence in the original article. It contains a very powerful concept; powerful, but taboo. Sorry, there is only one solution — banish it irrevocably. However, "the power classes" can be softened by substituting "the socially and politically dominant classes".

Lesson eight

Retain all abstract words and add others for effect wherever possible. For example, retain "remediation", "unitary achievement", "juxtapositions", "transactional mode" and "sophisticated metalanguage". Then turn "school environments" into "instructional environments" and "covering up" into "concealment".

Lesson nine

Learn to telescope. In the printing game, words are money. There's a bit of a problem here because sometimes the reader has to think harder when the editor telescopes. As you know, this runs counter to the sentiments of lesson three. Nevertheless, the "rule economic" overrides all others.

If the writer wishes the reader to follow the Odyssey of his thoughts into some off-beat paths, then let him write novels. Educational journals have room only for clear-cut expressways.

Lesson ten

Any living human twitches and the warts and blemishes on the body of the work must be disguised. The editor/mortician has to see to it that the body is beautifully composed in rest, worshipful, cosmetically perfected, the illusion of life in death. Dried floral arrangements are preferred. And no body should be offered up without due acknowledgment of the forebears, bibliographically chronicled.

If you would be an apprentice in the parlour of illusions, learn to expunge, "I think", "I wonder", "Why?", and "How?" Reduce to a minimum "probably" and "seems" and "perhaps". Let the educator's image come near to that of God (or deputy God), and remember, God does not speculate, nor does he wonder. God knows. He never has hunches.

By the way, an interesting tomb-like, prophetic, distant quality can be effected in the voice if you use the right filters.

You say you have not neutralized my style. Can you absorb my lessons and still make that assertion? Why didn't you send me back the original and say what you meant? Then I could have helped. I can now look at the offending piece and see many things to change (and tighten). Any piece of writing is at best an armistice with your other self, the reader over your own shoulder. I reckon I could now make war on it much better than you have. After all, I know the enemy pretty well. But you didn't afford me the courtesy of fighting my own battle. Like so many arrogant English teachers before you, you had to pre-empt my learning experience to feed your own ego.

The first three pages are full of ideas leaping around confusedly. Nevertheless they keep coming back to the central theme. That's the way I like to let myself into my thinking. I circle around the core a little, measure it up from various perspectives and then find a good way in. It is my conceit that the reader will be helped if he knows the way I think. His response will be quite different if he realizes that he is dealing with a discursive diverger (if that's what I am) and not a conventionally logical thinker.

I want to be vulnerable to my reader's criticism. I want to say "here I am; take what you find interesting; discard the rest". I don't want my writing to be merely functional. If I can somehow capture some of the rhythms and tones of speech it may be that my reader will feel some of my anger, some of my fear, some of my excitement, some of my uncertainty. If I cast out a wide net of words and ideas, I may help my reader (as well as myself) to catch more meanings, not the same meaning.

What is more, educational articles only achieve fame if there are plenty of leading educators to misunderstand them. I want to be misunderstood; to be understood is to die . . .

If you haven't already guessed, I refuse to have my work, so edited, published in your journal.

Returning to your latest letter, I am saddened. You refuse to acknowledge me as a person. You diminish me. Stolidly you have built a fortress wall of official words and on the steps of status and national importance you ceremoniously ascend to the top. Thereon you stand at a great height and with the aid of tongs proceed to urinate on me.

On that note, I leave you still quizically exposed. And if you are thinking of editing the above, might I suggest a two word imperative common amongst the more vulgar of us.

Yours *sincerely*,
GARTH BOOMER.

P.S. Please don't take this personally."

Looking back on that last letter, I have now lost the pleasure I then had in penning the final taunts. I could have been a little more subtle. But I meant them at the time. You see, I had come to feel what many kids must feel when cold teachers coldly mark something they really wanted to say.

The difference between those kids and me is that I had the words and the self-confidence to retaliate. Yet, notice now my conditioning to euphemism kept me from the clear, direct Anglo-Saxon insult I really wanted to use.

On a calmer note I wrote the last sad letter on 18 April 1975:

"Dear . . . . . .,

I wish to bring to an end the continuing correspondence between you and me, with this note.

You may be sure that I regret what has happened. Perhaps, if the first letter I received had been as tactful as the last, none of the fuss would have happened.

I have stood on a principle, a very simple but profound principle — that each human being is entitled to his own voice. You proposed to take mine away. I protested; you seemed not to hear. In the letter you have just received, you will hear me shouting so that you will hear.

On the quality and the effectiveness of my article I am prepared to concede that it is rough around the edges. You don't seem to understand why I wanted it this way.

So . . . I regret but, since I have also learnt, I rejoice.

Yours sincerely,

GARTH BOOMER."

I've got to be me 23

What follows is a selection from one cassette tape sent to Jean and Catherine and Simon and me in London from Mum and Dad in Littlehampton, Australia. My father, affectionately known as "Grumpy", spoke without interruption for about three quarters of an hour.

He'd never used a tape recorder before we went to London.

He was amazed when I asked whether I could put him in a book, but he eventually agreed.

"If you're bloody silly enough, I might as well be the same."

To get best value from it, read it aloud with a broad Australian accent.

Harold Rosen said in an introduction to some of the transcripts which he published in the magazine, *Language and Class:*

"Guil is a remarkable talker; we might call him a virtuoso. Speech flows effortlessly from him. What is even more remarkable about him is the total comfort with which he composes letter-tapes to his son, Garth, and grandchildren in England. Unfortunately, some of his more impressive qualities leak out of the transcript; his range of tone, variations of speech, management of voice quality and ability to express feeling all have to be guessed at. What is certainly left, however, amongst much else is his ability to adjust his style to different listeners without any feed-back . . . whether he is talking to the children or the adults, he can represent in language the texture of everyday life. A whole philosophy emerges from the full tapes."

A Yack on the Tape

"Righto. Here we go. Guess who. Way you go, too.

Well, that 'Way you go' was for your mother. She's here setting me up to have a little bit of a yack on the tape. Head supervisor, organiser and that was that. She's left me here. I'm in the lounge and with a cup of coffee at me elbow.

As usual I've been up the garden trying to do something. And I've been thinking of you, Catherine, while I was up there, and Simy and I thought,

'Now, when are those kids coming back? They're coming back next Christmas.'

So I dug a bit of ground and I had a look around the strawberry bushes and there was some nice runners on them and I thought 'Well, now I better put them out in the ground, and see if I can get some to grow so as when Simon and Catherine comes home next Christmas, there'll be some strawberries for them . . .'"

That's the Way She Is

"We've had plenty of strawberries — any amount. Nan's made little pots of jam. Every week she'd make three or four or five pots of jam. Guess what we did with 'em? We didn't eat 'em.

Oh well, Maxine'd like a few of these, a little bit of this jam. I'll take a few out to Davy Crockett. He likes it on his toast and Bernice might like some.

So, poor old Nan. Buys the sugar; picks the strawberries; makes the jam, gives it away and then she's real happy. That's the way she's built and that's the way she is."

Beautiful Mushrooms

"Last night . . . about yesterday afternoon 'bout half past three, I said to Nan, 'I think I'll go out and see if I can get a few mushrooms for tea.'

So I jumped in the little green bomb and away we go out towards Ron Norris' place. And I got out in the paddock there and I don't know . . . I s'pose I found about five pounds. They were beautiful mushrooms.

So I come home and got in about — oh I don't know — must have bin gittin' on to five o'clock . . . So Rita said, 'Well, we gunna have some f' tea?' So we both set sail and we peeled a great big panful of mushrooms — beautiful mushrooms and so we had our first mushrooms for the season and they were beautiful and we've got enough left for tea tonight.

I peeled them this morning. After I had me breakfast, I peeled 'em so we've got a great big panful for Nan and I for tea.

Auntie Elm's over here at the moment . . . and your Nan was goin' to give her some f' tea. But when I was up the garden just a minute ago there was a 'peep, peep . . . peep, peep, peep' and I thought 'O.K., who the hell is that.' I couldn't see who was peeping to me and I looked up the back road and there was Jim Miels and his wife sitting in the car.

So up I saunter and they said, 'How many mushrooms did you get last night?'. I said, 'Who told you I went mushrooming?'. 'Oh, well' he said, 'Elmie did.' 'Well' I said, ' we've been out and we've just got three plastic buckets full' and he had them there in the car. And he said, 'D' you want some?' and I said, 'No. I got enough peeled fr tea f' tonight.' I said, 'I'll tell you what, though; Elmie being yr neighbour, she likes them and a . . . ours are peeled f' tea tonight. She's not gittin' those. You give her some of yours for a feed tonight.'

So Auntie Elm's goin' to get some. Jim said. 'I'll give everybody in the cottages some. 'Cause (he said) I only want enough for a couple of feeds' and he had three milk buckets full. Beautiful mushrooms. Not the big type. Nice brown ones: no insects; lovely and pink and all. He did tell me where he got them, too. So if I want a few, I'll step out tomorrow morning and get some. Because they won't last very long. As soon as the cold weather comes, that'll be the end of that. Then we'll only get those odd great big ones. But these are terrific mushrooms and so I hope you're having some too in London.

I don't know whether your mother likes them Catherine or not or whether you like them, but I know your Daddy, he likes them. And I wish you were all here to have a feed with us tonight. And when we have our tea tonight we'll be thinking of you all the while.

Tucker

We haven't got much in Australia going for us at all, nothing at all bar tucker and we've got tucker. If we haven't got money we've got tucker. We've never had money all our lives but we've always had tucker. Plenty of it and good tucker and it's still on. You know Nan. You can't beat her. You couldn't beat her . . . for tucker."

* * *

"It wasn't a very nice day here, Anzac Day, anyway, for more reasons than one. I'll tell you why directly. . . ."

The White Cliffs of Dover

"We went to Wallaroo together. That was a good ding in a way.

Don wants to sit up and booze on and we went to bed on him at Wallaroo and he hasn't forgotten it.

He sent me a bottle of beer for me birthday and said it was cooled in the waters of the White Cliffs of Dover.

There is a big old heap of slag at Wallaroo, old black stuff, out of the mines or something, and so every time we used to drive past that whilst we were at Wallaroo I used to sing:

'There'll be bluebirds over
The White Cliffs of Dover'   (*sings*)

And of course bein' 'alf tiddly every time we passed the White Cliffs of Dover, he said 'By Jesus', he said, 'I'll tell Aral about that; you singin' *The*

White Cliffs of Dover.' He said 'She'll laugh her head off because she absolutely hates the sight of that black heap . . .'"

On Me Own

"You reckon that I was training off the tape. Well I s'pose, if you know our house as well as I do and you do, there's always somebody here and something going on. And you can't talk with the gang around . . . I can't. I got to get away on me own and then I've got to be me, which I'm not allowed to be most of the time . . . I come in and have a bash and 'no, that's got to be talked over.' Now you'll get to know what I mean by regimentated, regimented and organized, one thing and another. If something's not just right, that's got to be talked over and then, well, I turn on an act and then I won't talk at all . . ."

The Biggest Clown

"I spoke to the old pommie Bert Bishop this morning, up in the shop (he's our local grocer) and said 'We got a tape from Garth, since he came back from Russia.' I said, 'Oh, I said, he got Vodkarged or something like that,' I said.

I have a bang at 'im every morning I go in about something. I said 'Who you bloody barrackin' for now', I said. 'I bet you're barracking for the West Indies. You're not barrackin' for the Aussies.'

And of course he rams for the Poms all the while we play, for the Poms and, of course, he'd ram for anybody else, Pakistan, West Indies or anybody to beat Aussies.

So we have a little bit of a set to each morning and his wife says to me when I'm leaving:

'Well', she says, 'Thanks, Mr. Boomer, for your morning laugh', she says.

I said, 'Yes', I said, 'that's alright. You get a morning laugh', I said. 'A bloody man asks for ten cents worth of credit, he wouldn't be able to get it.'

Well, that makes her laugh more. She looks for my going up to get the mail and the paper each morning and I really get her giggly.

She reckons I'm the biggest clown or comedian around the place. Never mind. They're good people. They treat us really well. And they know their good customers. Their cash customers."

Fillet Steak

"I cooked a barbecue the other day for the gang . . . Auntie Pearl was here. Rose was here. Elmie was here, Dennis was here, Helen and the kids were all here, and I was a bit of a busy boy. But we got through. Mother has beautiful fillet steak . . . Just to show how financial she is, I s'pose she had that 'bout a dollar twenty a pound, I think, but anyhow that's nothing. I took some to Wallaroo too and it was, it was real snodger. There's nothing like fillet steak, cut in nice thick chunks. Not quite as rare as you like it, Garth, though, it wasn't. But everyone declared it was beautiful. It was, too, and we had chops and we had snags, and we had eggs. Mother kept it warm in the stove and everybody had to sit down. Personally, I like a barbecue out in the open with a lump in me 'and and a glass of ale in the other."

The Benefit of the Doubt

"The league football's in full swing again. You wouldn't have any news of that I shouldn't think.

Oh, the sad thing I was going to tell you was a very bad day on Anzac Day. I said the weather wasn't good and something worse than that happened. Well, the thing that was worse than that that happened was that North got toppled. Port beat them.

The Cocko's played the Port Adelaide's on the Adelaide Oval. It was a really ding dong go but Port's run it out a little bit better than the Cocko's. The Cocko's are short of a couple of good ruckmen and Patterson got reported. Went before the tribunal last night but they gave him the benefit of the doubt. He should have got matches in my opinion. I'm a realist really. He ran at a bloke and kneed him in the guts and then somebody come in to fix him and he hit him under the jaw as well as (*laughter*) he dobbed Cahill, he hit Cahill in the guts, Johnny Cahill, (he's still playing), and in comes Spencer to have a ping a Patterson and he hit him under the chops too.

Oh, previous to that, last week, Phillipou, one of the Eagles (they're a rough dirty lot of cows they are, and when I say that I'm not saying it just for fun either. This year, they're terrible, they're the roughest mob in the game).

But anyway, Peter Phillipou kicked somebody and he got four matches. First report in his whole career. He admitted that his boot did make contact with this player. I don't know who it was now.

But he said that he didn't deliberately kick him. Well perhaps, he didn't.

But Patterson should have got a couple whether or not. He might have been under provocation but that doesn't put the milk in the coconut."

Yellow Yolks and Silver Beet

"My pullets, Catherine, my little chickens, they're laying beautifully. I've got eleven pullets plus some old ones. They're in the moult, the old ones but my little pullets; they're laying beautifully and your Daddy would like to have some of their eggs because they've got nice yellow yolks and they get plenty of silver beet to eat to keep their yolks nice and I get about eight eggs from the 'leven of them. So you can see they're going top hole, really top hole.

And they know me. They like me and I talk to them and they say, 'Cok, cok, cok, cok' and if you was here, Sime, they'd say 'Come on Simon, get my googie. There's a brown one in the corner there.'

I've got a little white fowl with black feathers and she talks too, and David's frightened to go and get the eggs. That's how big a sook he is. He's a big boy. But you'd go in and get them wouldn't you Sime? And you'd count 'em into the tin — one, two, free, four and take them down to Nan and put 'em in the dish . . . Yeh.

I don't know whether they're a paying proposition. I don't think they are. They lay well . . . you know how it goes."

Value for Money

"I'm only a lazy old bludger. I don't do very, very little. Well, I can't. I'm not too, too fit. Although just to give you a little bit of an idea that I can go just a tiny little bit, I went back to work the week before Easter. They said, 'You might want a quid for Easter.' And I went back and done a week's work back there. It was just as much as I could do, too, but I surprised meself. When you're away from work you lose confidence in yourself and you think, 'Well, I can't do that. I'd get giddy here and giddy there', which I do all the damn time. I think if I go back to work, I'll fall arse over head, but, no I went back and they got value for money."

It's You all Over

"I just don't know what I could say to the kids. I think of them all the time.

I liked your tape Catherine. You're a little bit of a magpie, Catherine.

If Simon's s'posed to say something you hop in and say it for him. But he won't co-operate anyway. I did enjoy him having a cry. I thought that was very nice. Do it more often Sime. Have a cry when the tape's going, when they're recording.

Jean, you can come into it too. And you can say 'I'll smack your bottom Simon!' It's you, it's you alright, it's you all over (*laughter*). Nice to hear your voice, Jean.

I reckon Grump's hogging the tape this time . . .

If I can get away on me own, I'll talk some bullshit alright."

The Life of the Party

"One of the brickyard employees' wife. It was on the Monday, yes, . . . the Monday before Easter, he was on steaming the kiln . . . Eric Wagett, it was, from Mt. Barker, and he went off at 8 o'clock and he went home and he found his wife dead in bed.

He left her at midnight and she was quite alright and he went home in the morning and she was gone . . . so that's very, very sad for him. He's a man just about fifty, a terrific worker, terrific worker. I haven't seen him. I wrote him a sympathy card, personally. I didn't go to the funeral because I don't think it does anything for me at this stage, going to funerals. I don't think it hurts me but probably it does stir me up a bit. Specially with a chap like him because I have great respect for him and knew his wife very well . . . from the dinners. She was the life of the party . . . you could have a bit of fun with her. You could tell her to go to buggery if you wanted to and she'd tell you the same. Well, that'd suit me, wouldn't it?"

A Gold Medal

"They get spoilt them damn kids. There's no doubt about that. But still that's Nan's whole life. She whacks the money out on them. She'd buy 'em anything.

Bloody fool could have plenty for herself if she wanted it. But she'd rather not have it for herslef. Not a selfish bone in her body, I'm afraid. Being in a selfish world, well, she's right out of place.

But we're still living together and I s'pose she should have a gold medal."

You've Got to Put Your Chin Out

"I went to the gas man, Cambridge, the other day and I said . . . Oh, I was up there when he was cleaning his boots going to work, that's how early I was there, 'bout half past seven.

And he said, "Ullo, what d' you want? Bottle of gas?' 'Oh' I said, 'I don't know whether I do or whether I don't', I said. 'I do but I don't know whether I do until I have a talk to you.'

He said, 'What's the trouble?' 'Well', I said, 'We've been quoted our . . .' I said, 'Ow much is a bottle of gas?' He said, "Leven dollars fifty'. 'Well, I said, 'Now listen, we're bloody pensioners. We got to make . . .' (I put over a bit of sob stuff). I said, 'We got to make every post a winning post', I said, 'and we've been quoted ten dollars against eleven fifty', I said. 'Well, a dollar fifty a bottle of gas is better in my pocket than in yours', I said. 'I'm not going to mention the person that quoted but it has been quoted to me.' 'Yeh,' he said, 'You needn't tell me who it is', he said. 'I'll give him a run for his bloody money directly, too'.

'Well', I said, 'Now, with people with two or three appliances they get theirs for nine dollars seventy five and all this sort of racket', I said. 'We've only got one I know, but we use more gas than them. Now what about you?'

'Well', he said, 'How much gas do you use?'. I said, 'I'd use six bottles from now till Christmas.' He said, 'If you can guarantee to me you'd use six bottles of gas, you can 'ave it for nine dollars seventy five . . .'

So I'm getting it for nine seventy five through opening me big trap. Whether I use six or not won't worry me. I'll get it on the cheap first.

So you've got to put your chin out a bit . . ."

* * *

Grumpy's Tape, as I now call it, is a delight to me.

I can't help wondering where I fit in. Grumpy's language calls me back, makes me feel at home, makes me chuckle, lets me in.

Now with many years of schooling and teaching behind me, I am trying to discover once again who I am. You see, my teachers taught me another language. They taught me, in good faith, because they knew what the examiner wanted, to relinquish my own voice in the service of academic learning. And I learnt well.

Because I lived outside school as well, I also kept some of the language of home and neighbourhood places where we laughed and sang and argued and talked. But a tension of which I was probably not even aware at that time had begun.

When I left the little village in the hills for the big city and the university, I guess I put away childish things. No longer "working class", I experienced the wilderness of no man's land, feeling terribly gauche and inferior amongst the lecturers, and always slightly funny when I went home and had a few drinks with my old friends in the local pub.

In all my time at school and university there were only a few teachers who let me in or helped me relax. But I played the games well and graduated. Since then, I think I've been steadily re-discovering myself and finding my own voice.

But I must not romanticize the language of home, Grumpy's language. A careful analysis does show seven small deviations from "accepted" syntax and purists will possibly object to "me" for "my".

(Funny how the working classes are said to be lazy and sloppy for dropping letters. What about the way English teachers drop their "r's" in "mother" and "father".)

I know I could never survive in my world with his language and I owe much to my education. It has given me an advantage that Grumpy does not have. In most cases now I know when those holding important stations in education are talking or writing crap. It takes one to know one. Grumpy would simply remain unaffected by learned language.

I think I owe my slowly returning sense of identity to the vigorous, loving, harsh, flexible, earthy language of home. I refused to be refined. School could not filter out my persistent vulgarity. In the end, I refused to be eternally on my guard not to break the rules or to betray the conventions.

Paradoxically, now that I know the games and the rules, I am free.

I can now laugh at Bernstein's notion of the restricted code and can acknowledge the genius of Grumpy who left school at twelve and spent most of his working life moulding bricks at the Littlehampton Brick Company.

Apart from a few years with the armed forces in Darwin, during the war, he has rarely travelled more than fifty miles from his day's circle. He prefers to stay at home where they talk the "restricted" "hillbilly" dialect with its handful of grammatical deviances.

As a teacher, he restricts himself to teaching his grandchildren how to play crib and switch and euchre. He also has a good bag of songs, jokes, riddles and "magical" tricks to keep them amused.

But I wonder what Grumpy would have done if instead of moulding bricks he had been asked to mould children; if instead of being conscripted to the army, he'd been conscripted to teaching?

I've got a hunch that the voice which reached so easily across 19 000 kilometres and made us all laugh in London, would have had little trouble in reaching to the child in the back row. Why then, in the past, have I been so eager to change so many kids?

You know, I wouldn't want to change Grumpy at all.